In the
Moods

When Bipolar Disorder and
Substance Dependence Intersect

MARLENE STOTLAND COHEN, PH.D., M.A.

&

GERALD J. MOZDZIERZ, PH.D.

PUBLICATIONS KEREN CHAI PUBLISHING

ALL ABOUT LIVING BRIGHT

DOLLARD DES ORMEAUX, QUEBEC
WESTERN SPRINGS, IL

PUBLICATIONS KEREN CHAI PUBLISHING
ALL ABOUT LIVING BRIGHT

Copyright © 2003 by Marlene Stotland Cohen & Gerald J. Mozdzierz

National Library of Canada Cataloguing in Publication

Cohen, Marlene Stotland, 1943-
        In the moods : when bipolar disorder and substance dependence intersect / by Marlene Stotland Cohen & Gerald J. Mozdzierz.

Includes bibliographical references.
ISBN 0-9734085-0-2

        1. Manic-depressive persons--Substance use--Popular works.
2. Manic-depressive illness--Diagnosis--Popular works. 3. Manic-depressive illness--Treatment--Popular works. 4. Substance abuse--Diagnosis--Popular works. 5. Substance abuse--Treatment--Popular works. 6. Adlerian psychology--Popular works. I. Mozdzierz, Gerald J., 1940- II. Title.

RC516.C63 2003   616.89'50651   C2003-905975-8

Library of Congress Control Number: 2003195122

Disclaimer and Limits of Liability:
The recommendations in this book are not to be considered as, or intended to replace medical or psychotherapeutic advice. Each person's mental health and physical condition needs to be assessed on an individual basis by a health care professional to determine an appropriate treatment plan for recovery. The authors, the publisher, and the distributors of this book shall not be liable to the purchaser or any other person or entity with respect to any damage or loss alleged to be caused directly or indirectly by the information contained in this book.
The authors have made every effort to ensure accuracy in the information contained in this book. They assume no responsibility for errors or omissions herein. Any slights of people, places or organizations are entirely unintentional.

Keren Chai Publishing
P.O. Box 38021
3353 Sources Blvd.
Dollard des Ormeaux, Quebec H9B 3J2

Editorial Department in the U.S.: Keren Chai Publishing, 5608 Western Springs, IL 60558
For Canada & USA orders: Please contact Keren Chai Publishing, P.O. Box 38021, 3353 Sources Blvd., Dollard des Ormeaux, Quebec H9B 3J2. Call toll free 1-866-404-6040; Fax: (514) 683-6235 (Lines are open from 9 a.m. to 5 p.m. Monday to Friday) or log onto our website: www.kerenchai.ca

Cover Design & Layout by Yossy Obadia
Printed and bound in Canada.

Contents

Acknowledgements

We are grateful to the many people who gave us the caring support we needed to bring this project to completion. On the top of our list, we acknowledge the dedication of our spouses, Elie and Charlene. All our immediate family members have participated in some way in the manuscript, and in like so many other areas of our lives, we thank them lovingly for being there for us as always.

Family, friends and colleagues were willing to read through the different versions of the manuscript. Their feedback has been constructive, encouraging, and invaluable. They are: Aaron Borek, Shirley Callender, Tom Caplan, Christine Clark, David Cohen, Penny Cohen, Stephen Cohen, Trudy Friedman, Giselle Goudreault, Rebecca Hart, Judy Kaback, Flora Kaplan, Silvija Leckman, Lawrence Lefcort, Mitchell Phomin, Amira Richler, Leonie Richler, and Gerry Singer.

It was a pleasure to work with Yossy Obadia on the graphics and layout of the book. We appreciate his talent and his good nature.

Being a coauthor can have its pitfalls, but we were very fortunate indeed to have the reciprocal support and respect of one another. The creation of *In the Moods* was a positive and fulfilling experience for both of us.

Shalom / Peace
Marlene Stotland Cohen & Gerry J. Mozdzierz

1
You and Moodcycling

If you're reading this book, you or someone you love or someone in your care probably suffers from so-called bipolar disorder. We used to call this troubling recurrent condition "manic-depressive illness" and we call a less intense version "cyclothymia". In this book, we'll call the whole constellation of conditions "moodcycling".

Moodcycling disorders are typically recurrent and characterized by extreme shifts in mood, energy level and functioning, often suddenly and unexpectedly emerging from a symptom-free state of wellness. Worldwide, between one and two percent of all people are affected. Men and women appear to suffer in equal numbers. A recent survey showed a rise in significant bipolar symptoms in 3.7 per cent of the United States population. Surprisingly, many of those affected — eighty per cent — are going undiagnosed, or misdiagnosed for depression. Higher rates of the disorder are being found between 18 to 24 year olds than ever before.

Of those with bipolar disorders, almost half are dependent on substances such as alcohol and drugs and the bipolar group is eleven times more likely to have such dependency than people in the general population. In recent years, we've come to recognize that this "dual diagnosis" of moodcycling and substance dependency is very common indeed. Some research has even suggested that the pattern of mood disorders, including substance abuse, can be passed down to the next generation, though alcohol and substance abuse might simply be, as New York psychiatrist Dr. Ronald Fieve has suggested, the sufferer's self-medication for anxiety and depression.

Let's look at that extremely moody individual in your family, at your place of work, or in your mirror. Moods can shift from euphoria and grandiosity to deep, black melancholy. Most people are familiar with depression, the melancholy side of moodcycling. Everyone at one time or another has had the winter blahs or felt life was a bummer. Perhaps we've experienced the deep sadness that follows the death of a loved one or the emptiness that can accompany the end of a relationship or the loss of a good job. But clinical depression is much more than that. When you're clinically depressed, you may feel worthless in a profound and sustained way, your level of energy may be debilitating low and you may completely lose interest in the ordinary activities of life, including such perennially fascinating subjects as sex and food. Your outlook for the present and the future is indescribably bleak. Your sleep patterns may be disrupted and you may feel continuously tired. You feel utterly inadequate. Your mental concentration is so impaired that you're no longer really productive in school, at work, at home. You might not be able to think in a clearly focused way. You might withdraw from social contact. You might resort to drugs or alcohol to give yourself some relief —the second part of the dual diagnosis — and this complicates your picture considerably. You might ponder ending your own life.

Manic behavior and moods, of course, are just the opposite — high, thoroughly energized, euphoric, elevated, expansive, and irritable. In the manic phase, you're on the go, full of energy, self-centered. You're the original cock-eyed optimist, full of ambitions and feelings of productivity, with some strange, self-imposed working hours and conditions to go along with those feelings. You don't need much sleep. You know you can accomplish just about anything. You indulge in excesses of all sorts, live on the edge and at the extremes. You're often talkative, with sharpened and unusually creative thinking, rushed and uncritical about your work. You don't like to do routine or unpleasant things. You're easily bored. You crave constant novelty. You're usually incapable of considering the consequences of any of these behaviors.

These poles of the bipolar condition have been long recognized and are often thought of as "brain chemistry" disorders. Many of us, though, are convinced that learned patterns of personality contribute to such seemingly "biochemical" illnesses. These patterns of behavior and thought, these interactions with others, difficult to change as they are, may be rooted in a personality disorder that was well-established and recognizable by adolescence. People who experience true moodcycling may have long felt unfulfilled and dissatisfied with the attention and recognition they've received from their family, their teachers, their friends, their associates at work. In their eyes, the behavior or performance of others may have failed to come up to expectations.

Whatever the root cause may turn out to be, we believe that the way in which individuals see themselves can inhibit or promote the healing process. There is a formidable amount of literature by clinicians indicating that counseling, in conjunction with specific medications, has an important role to play in the treatment of this dual diagnosis condition. That's why we call to our aid a most unusual caregiver, one who probably never heard the words "bipolar disorder" used together, but who has much to teach us nonetheless.

Viennese psychiatrist Alfred Adler was born in 1870, only fourteen years after the birth of Freud. He died in 1937. Adler had an outstanding interest in social problems and social betterment. His theories and their applications grew into what is now called Individual Psychology, a discipline that recognizes the uniqueness of each human being. Adler was the first to develop a comprehensive theory of personality that emphasized the social "embeddedness" that is, connectedness, of people. Individuals, he taught, behave or react according to their unique interpretations of themselves and their interactions with others and the world around them. His approach allowed for comprehensive glimpses into how children develop their place in their families and how those children, grown to adults, fare in the social world as a result. Adler's great interest in family and other socially based groups led him to organize some of the first community-outreach programs for child guidance and family education.

Adler would have looked at maladjustments such as bipolar disorder and substance abuse from a humanistic and holistic perspective that centered on children and family life. He avoided putting labels on people. The maladjustment of the individual, he taught, arises from feelings of inferiority about oneself, from a decrease in social interest and from the development of an uncooperative goal of superiority. In these cases, and unless the suffering individual is challenged by a major life experience or some form of psychotherapy, he or she will attempt to solve problems using a self-centered and unconscious strategy. Adler felt that a person's unique belief system represents the core of his or her personality and is the key to understanding the unique individual. For Adler, a democratic sense of warmth and fairness enveloped his assessment of every patient.

But as someone afflicted with a bipolar disorder or a substance dependence — or as a family member or friend of such a person — you may still doubt whether a connection exists between Adler's insights into the mechanism of human personality and these baffling disorders that may have a neurochemical component at their root.

First, remember that mood disorders and addictions are, at one level, afflictions like any other, whether suffered before birth or afterwards. We might think of them as we think of the loss of an arm. Whether an individual was born without an arm or lost it later, its absence constitutes a challenge that must be met. Part of the strength we require to face any challenge comes from a better understanding of ourselves, a better inventory of the tools at our disposal. Psychotherapy or counseling offers the hope of developing awareness. Adlerian psychology specifically may allow us to see how hobbled we may be by a faulty style of life. In this way psychotherapy helps us solve the problems of living — even the problems posed by a disease — through common sense and increased social interest.

But going beyond this general truth, many present-day Adlerian psychologists agree that there are problems in what they call the "life tasks" of people diagnosed with the dual diagnosis of bipolar disease and substance abuse. These problems can be addressed by psychotherapy and psychotherapy has been shown to be as powerful a treatment tool as the psychoactive drugs that have garnered so much acclaim in recent decades. Why should we deny ourselves such a tool, then, when it comes parceled with greater personal understanding, something no drug claims to possess?

It is often said that there are no two snowflakes alike and that the same is true for the personality of human beings. But as therapists, our experience is that Dr. Adler was right. We share in common the development of cognitive patterns that are formed in early childhood, including our faulty convictions. It is no more than common sense that these belief systems may help sustain the misery of mood disorders and substance abuse, whatever their cause. When we look at the whole person and the problems they face in meeting life's tasks, when we encourage a person to establish new, pro-social goals and address neglected areas of his or her life, when we encourage behavior change in those who display symptoms of moodcycling, we empower the one who has the most to gain. Can the patterns of thought and the behavior formulated in childhood be unmasked and then linked to these mood swings and drug use in adult life? These are the areas in question that we'll address in this book.

A last point: psychotherapy is only one facet of our approach to these disorders. We've already mentioned medication, and the famous 12-step programs such as those offered by Alcoholics Anonymous or Al-Anon have also proven useful in helping people recover from problems and symptoms related to substance abuse and alcoholism. These programs have much in common with Adler's principles. Along with various family and group therapies, they offer family, friends and colleagues the support and understanding they need if they are to usefully support a loved one suffering from a mood disorder. Insight, medication, and rehabilitation — all play a part.

For those of you afflicted with these disorders, it probably goes without saying that the first and necessary ingredient in the changing of any behavior or mental health problem is the strong desire to help yourself. If you have chosen to read this book, you are expressing such a desire. This book is about hope and health. The struggle against mental disorders is indeed a great challenge. Patients find themselves disabled at a most fundamental level. Families strive to unite behind a most elusive foe and summon the widest range of personal resources. But it is our hope that these pages, with Dr. Adler on one side and you on the other, can open a door to your further understanding and health.

2
The Ideas of Alfred Adler

The Healthy Personality

Alfred Adler saw the individual human being as part of a larger system — the family, the community, all of humanity, the planet, even the cosmos — and he believed that a sense of this social connectedness gave direction to a person's actions, what he called "useful striving" — constructive, but innovative. This idea comprises the distinctive cornerstone of his thinking.

We may be born to some degree with the capacity for this sense of community that Adler describes, but he felt that it was largely something that has to be developed from a young age through the guidance and persistence of family members and teachers. A person learned to use common sense, based on reality, in order to contribute to society in a useful way. Children do not have a broad understanding of life, of the world, or of human nature. They can be vulnerable to arriving at limited, faulty conclusions about their experiences — their "private logic" — that develops before a child can verbalize it, before age eight.

Adler believed that the mind, the body and the spirit of each individual are expressed through the acting, thinking and feeling of that person. These six components are interconnected and result in our forming convictions about ourselves, convictions that Adler called our "chosen style of life". Our style of life — linked with our creative capacity and intertwined with biological, social and environmental factors over which we have no control — helps us to compensate for our feelings of inferiority and insecurity. The child creates a road map that will assist him or her in coping *with* the world and provide a sense of belonging *in* the world. As social beings, we supply meaning to things in relation to other people in order to find that unique place of belonging that becomes our personal goal. Once the belief system of a person is understood, the underlying goal of his or her thoughts and behavior becomes clearer.

Adler disliked categorizing, but he did recognize that categories help us master new ideas. He suggested that we can roughly identify people's styles of life into themes. Clearly, a few pithy words represent an oversimplification of how someone sees themselves and cannot do justice to a person's self-concept. But once recognized — the person's behavior can be examined for its consistency with these life style themes.

One generalized style-of-life conviction involves the evaluation of self. Adler taught that this self-concept is an individual's interpretation of how he or she sees himself or herself. Examples of these are: "I am different (from everyone else)" or "I am unlovable" or "I am small and weak" or "I am big and strong" or "I am shy". It is a conclusion that a child reaches about herself or himself, distilled from experience, and it represents a powerful psychological inclination that sets the tone for childhood behaviors.

Subjective convictions that individuals may hold about the world and about the meaning of life in general are another style-of-life theme: "Life is fantastic" or "Life is hell on earth" or "Life offers me no opportunities" are examples of the distorted misperceptions of life and its demands. Again, a person develops an impression about life in early childhood. This basic orientation varies from individual to individual depending upon the experiences each has had and the interpretation each has made of those experiences. Even when siblings are raised under common living conditions, each may see life differently.

Life-style convictions can also depict distorted attitudes about people. "People are hostile" or "People are stupid" or "People are smarter than me" are examples of these perceptions shaping a person's interactions with others.

Other style-of-life convictions pertain to the "methods of operation" people have with themselves and in relation to others. For example, "I'm going to rebel against authority! I'll show them!" or "Others need to take care of me" or "I need to keep my distance from others and life's responsibilities."

When there is a difference between the actual self-convictions and the ideal self-convictions, feelings of inferiority develop. For example, an individual thinking "I am tall; I should be shorter", allows the person to feel inferior. Inferiority feelings also result when the convictions in the self-concept are incongruent with the picture the individual has about the world. For example, "I am weak, life is dangerous". We may also develop distorted ideals that shape our style of life by over generalizing our values and convictions. We might think, "The only thing worth being is a star! Either that or a genius!" or "A real man can drink a *lot* of beer" or "A real woman is so admired, people give her gifts every day" or "One should *always* tell the truth, but *I* lie".

When incongruities arise between our self-concept and these ethical convictions, we can have feelings of inferiority or guilt. The self-created goal and the developing life scripts might look like these examples: "I am small and weak. Life is dangerous for me. Others have to protect me." Or like this: "I am different from the rest. People are hostile and life is scary. Therefore, I need to be on top and one up on everyone else".

These styles of life shape our striving towards our — perhaps unrecognized — goals or ideals. They allow each of us to formulate our individual goal in a process of courageous striving towards an ideal universal community. We move through life, Adler taught, by ceaselessly striving, through the free exercise of our will, towards this private goal. The goal informs all our actions and we develop a dominant pattern that directs our lives, a dynamic force that points us, we hope, to a distinctive place in the world, to self-esteem, to a better way of life. But this self-created goal — our self-ideal, our personal fiction — is often unknown to us and unrecognized by those around us.

Perhaps surprisingly, these feelings of inferiority are not necessarily abnormal or unhealthy. In fact, they can spur us on to live out life by striving for *more* rather than surrendering to *less*. This striving in turn can allow us to interact with and adapt to the human environment and to become socially useful. But we rely on the "map" that our style of life provides to move forward through life and help us cope with our experiences. When we become aware of what's written on that map, we become more flexible in the choices we can make about our actions. We can be free to respond in new ways as the situation changes. The socially useful personality is cooperative and humble. Life's accomplishments generate a feeling of value and happiness that overrides feelings of inferiority. Adler originally outlined three areas of such accomplishment, which he called "life tasks". Present-day Adlerians describe two additional tasks of life.

The first life task is the "self task", that is, coping with one's self and being one's own best friend. It is the relationship between the "I" and the "me" of the individual. The second task is the "social task", that is, a person's level of social interaction between the "I" with the "you": friends, family, community, and the society at large. Teaching interpersonal skills related to friendship and community can equip the very young child to move through life engaged in striving to make the world a better place.

The third task is the "work task", that is, the degree to which a person's job is a positive force in their life, since work is essential for survival. This task also entails our interdependency on each other's labors. The fourth task is the "love (intimacy) task", based on a person's ability to interrelate to and cooperate with another in the context of a loving relationship. Through this task, the individual forms strong, committed and intimate ties with the family and a partner that may lead eventually to the development of a new family.

The fifth is the "spiritual task", and is about learning to define the nature of the universe and learning to relate to a Higher Power in the cosmos. We have learned through Alfred Adler that people who enjoy good mental health participate in all of these life tasks.

3
Psychotherapy and Adler

You may find Alfred Adler's vision of the healthy human personality, as we encountered it in Chapter 2, to be a convincing and even charming one. But can such ideas really help someone suffering from an emotional disorder?

Adler actually developed his theories of the human personality in the course of treating patients, that is, in the course of what we now call psychotherapy. And you may be surprised to learn that psychotherapy has a *proven* role to play in helping defeat mental and emotional illness, including the dual menace of moodcycling and substance dependence. We now have a body of respected work that can guide us in the treatment of these disorders using Adlerian strategies.

In this chapter we'll look briefly the main contributions to psychotherapy in modern times, and then at the compassionate and insightful approach taken by Adler, the first clinician to emphasize man's social embeddedness.

I.
The Development of Psychotherapy

Through most of the history of Western cultures, mental illness was treated by neglect or quarantine, much as leprosy was treated and with about as much foundation in fact. There was little progress towards a systematic and scientific (or at least rational) approach to mental and emotional illness until the work of Sigmund Freud in Vienna at the turn of the last century. Freud, whom most of us recognize as the father of the "talk therapy" known as psychoanalysis, provided the major role model for a century of therapists to follow. Freud's theories constituted a true breakthrough and have undoubtedly helped countless people, but Freud himself was something of an isolationist, and not particularly comfortable interacting with his patients face to face. He preferred that they lay on a couch with their eyes closed and he wrote notes as they talked, though usually he offered neither question nor comment. The psychoanalytic theory of the human personality that he developed, although its influence has been enormous, was not at all easy for his patients to understand.

Freud not only introduced the idea of the unconscious — something we take for granted today — but the idea that the unconscious was influenced by bodily drives — the human tendency to seek pleasure and avoid pain, the so-called pleasure principle. This pleasure principle was supposed to be predominant during a person's earliest years and was linked to the development of the "libido", the energy of the sexual drive. Freud believed the libido, at work in the unconscious, to be the cause of mental conflicts. Entailed in this was the notion that the conscious person was a helpless victim with no control.

In the wake of Freud's work and those of his disciples, several associated schools of psychotherapy subscribed to the idea of the unconscious. Adler, who had been a colleague of Freud's, owed some debt to Freud's basic tenet that the functioning of the mind is related to the functioning of the body. But Adler's far more humanistic ideas and observations emphasized that the unconscious is influenced by subjective values, interests and feelings that override such factors as environment, innate disposition and objective experience. Adler maintained, in other words, that the self was active and creative in the development of the personality and mental health. Adler believed in the individual's power of making choices and his work was to quietly permeate modern psychological thinking.

Following the development of talk therapies, the second breakthrough in the treatment of many mental and emotional illnesses came with the discovery in the 1950's and 1960's of anti-psychotic medicines and tranquilizers, and the somewhat later development of effective antidepressants. Psychiatrists soon began to rely heavily on the prescription of these medications to treat their patients. Recent studies suggest that medication may account for 25% (not 100% as some people mistakenly believe) of the behavioral changes that can take place in a therapeutic setting. But such medication has several drawbacks: not only are undesirable side effects common, but many people resist taking drugs for fear of these unwanted side effects. And, as the decades have passed, it has become evident that medication has not replaced "talk" therapy, which still accounts for a large percentage of observable changes in a therapeutic setting.

A third and immensely influential development was the rise of the cognitive behavioral schools of psychology in the 1960's and 1970's. These theories, which often produced convincing clinical results, suggested that how people felt was influenced by what and how they thought, and by changes in behavior. These "new" ideas were strikingly similar to the teachings of Alfred Adler a generation earlier.

II.
Adler's Contribution

Alfred Adler, as we've said, believed that the creative self can intervene to influence hereditary and environmental factors. He believed that a person's response to those factors determines his or her behavior. Each person may have the power to overcome and compensate for many weaknesses. A child, or even an adult, might develop an artistic talent that compensates for, say, poor vision.

But there are situations that can overburden a child and encourage the development of a faulty style of life. When children are discouraged or neglected, when they are unwanted or traumatized, when they have grave physical handicaps or are given too much responsibility — under these circumstances they can lose heart. On the other hand, children can be "under-burdened" — pampered or overprotected — with similar results. In this way, feelings of inferiority can develop in childhood that can lead to great maladjustment in life. These "neurotic" maladjustments can take the form of depression, mood swings or substance abuse.

Adler maintained that neurotic patients — and this term can extend to people suffering from bipolar and substance abuse disorders — retain a grasp on reality (something that psychotic patients often cannot do) but they hesitate in their life tasks —they become less productive. A neurotic person's goals will be more self-centered and these goals, Adler believed, may overlie an individual's feelings of inferiority, for which she or he unconsciously aims to compensate. It is from this part of Adler's theories that the term "inferiority complex" stems.

When a person acts *as if* he or she is inferior, the ensuing inferiority complex causes the person to openly demonstrate an inadequacy or a "sickness". Such people may make less of a contribution to society, suffer personal maladjustment and unhappiness, and feel incomplete as individuals. Psychological disorders and social failure, Adler taught, are the result of an individual's insufficient social feeling.

Although Adler believed that a total understanding of the personality meant understanding a person's predisposing biological factors — their genetic defects, handicaps, physical disease and so on — his hallmark remained his interest in his patients' social interactions and their private and unconscious goals. His observations led him to the belief that healthy persons were able to move through life and perform their life tasks by employing common sense and courage. Many of his patients who suffered from "psychopathologies" — mental and emotional illnesses — were characterized by selfish goals, not those that benefited others.

Discouragement, the creation of faulty conceptions and lifestyle beliefs had led to personality dysfunction and underdeveloped social interactions with the outside social world. Adler looked at his patients' symptoms through a holistic "prism of lifestyle" and became convinced that these symptoms should not be classified or categorized, but rather seen as unique constellations of behavior and attitude. His idea of therapy was to study and understand this unique pattern and to determine what purpose lay behind it.

How did he go about this?

Getting to know you

With his pioneering zest, Dr. Adler saw his patients a century ago in all kinds of settings, though most therapy was done in his office, and he invariably treated his patients as equals. He often began the therapy with the question: "Where would you like to sit?" How far away the patient chose to sit was an indication of his or her fear, or unwillingness, or hesitation to participate. This single question allowed Adler to establish a rapport and determine his patient's willingness to enter therapy. Provided this rapport was established, Adler felt it was possible to grasp the patient's "neurotic system" within the first day of meeting.

Present-day Adlerian therapists, following Adler's example, collect their patients' historical data, especially details of the patient's childhood years. They watch closely for body language, and listen carefully for what the patient is thinking and feeling. On this basis, the therapist strives to formulate the guiding lines and self-chosen direction that the patient has set — his or her "style of life". Adlerian therapy is meant to be an encouraging venture. Through uncovering and interpreting, therapists strive to help patients towards self-understanding.

You'll recall our discussion of the five life tasks from Chapter 2. These are the aspects of life that Adler recognized as critical to emotional health. These tasks are: relating to others through friendship and community involvement; making a contribution in school and/or work; achieving intimacy in love, marriage and parenting; getting along with oneself (that is, being aware of oneself); and developing the spiritual dimension, by which we mean developing values and developing a sense of life's goals in relationship to the universe or cosmos.

So one of an Adlerian therapist's goals may be to assess a patient's emotional health by determining how involved they are in each of their life tasks, or how distant they are from those tasks. The therapist assesses, for instance, how well the person is doing in school and at work. If there are problems in these areas, it is usually an issue of low self-esteem. This investigation goes forward in a therapeutic atmosphere of mutual trust.

Adlerian analysis often begins with an interview that is not necessarily structured, but does explore the crisis that brought the patient into therapy. "Let's imagine," the therapist might say, "that I have a magic wand, and you could be completely well by the time you left this office. What would you do differently than before?" Depending on the patient's answer, the therapist is able to determine if the problem is psychogenic or organic in nature.

The object of such a question is to determine the purpose that underlies the patient's complaints. Adlerians believe that "neurotic" illness makes sense — that there is a psychological superstructure, a logic, a private logic, that will be revealed by the patient's answer, regardless of any actual organic pathology. Physical complaints must be ruled out through lab tests and medical examination. But many such complaints are neurotic in origin and do not necessarily have an organic basis.

The therapist sets as a goal the daunting task of helping uncover the mystery of what makes the person tick.

Adlerians also look carefully at the patient's birth order amongst the siblings in the family and assess the development and movement of the patient within his or her family setting. They want to learn about parents, siblings, and any extended family, as well as the patient's description of himself or herself as a child growing up in that family. They recognize that this "family constellation" may influence the patient's style of life and personal mythology.

In the same way, the therapist will want to learn about the patient's school, about friends and hobbies, physical handicaps, and early recollections and dreams. Of course, the personal interaction between patient and therapist is itself a valuable source of clues.

Making Sense

After gathering specific material elicited in the diagnostic therapeutic sessions, the therapist's job becomes one of putting the material together and interpreting it in a way that will help the patient gain personal understanding. While Adlerians are concerned with how their patients feel and why they feel that way, they are even more concerned with helping the patient to discover the purpose or goals behind their behavior or attitudes — the purpose or goal behind their patients' movements and intentions. Categorizing this goal behind the behavior in question can serve as a valuable tool that helps us grasp the essentials of the life style, as mentioned in Chapter 2.

If the therapy is to be successful — if, that is, the patient is to correct his or her difficulties in the social environment of the world, if the patient is to self-actualize and grow — he or she must now put into practice the deeper understanding or insight learned in the course of therapy. When a patient has recognized the goals and faulty logic underlying his or her behavior, the therapist provides support and encouragement until the patient is at last aware of his or her power to act constructively and make decisions, understanding that he or she has the freedom to choose his or her own direction and is not stuck in the child-like patterns formed while growing up in the family of origin.

During this stage of re-education and reorientation, the Adlerian therapist may look with their patients at their life tasks and encourage more constructive involvement in each. In the area of personal regard, for instance, increasingly self-aware patients will become less negative and less hard on themselves, and perhaps develop the ability to laugh at themselves when they recognize they are going back to the old patterns. In interactions with family and loved ones, they may learn how to communicate more effectively, even assertively, look upon relationships more favorably and sustain more positive interactions. They may learn to reach out to friends and support groups more often and become less negative and more productive by learning to communicate more effectively at work or at school. At a spiritual level, they may begin to sense that they are not alone in the cosmos.

Education, awareness and training in all the life tasks may allow an afflicted person to let go of the preoccupation with self and open the door to a profound feeling of belonging and a genuine interest in the welfare of others. The development of this social adjustment, belated though it may be, can come about with the help of family members, life partners, friends, work associates, a spiritual community, a psychotherapist, others in helping professions, and, most important of all, the patient.

4
The Dual Diagnosis

I.
Understanding the Problem

We know more today about how the mind works — normally and abnormally — than at any other time in history. The variety of psychotherapies and theories can be bewildering, but a common thread in many is the classification system of mental illnesses formulated by the American Psychiatric Association in a reference book called the Diagnostic and Statistical Manual of Mental Disorders (DSM). The search for clarity has become so acute that the original DSM has been expanded eight times in the last 50 years.

The current DSM-IV standardizes symptoms and evaluates mental problems from a medical, psychological and social perspective. Appendix 1 and 2 of this book lists the DSM-IV's diagnosis and breakdown of symptoms present in bipolar disorder and substance dependence. You might look through them to see if you or your loved one shows these signs. They are there for your information, but don't neglect to make an appointment with a qualified health care professional if you feel you have a problem you cannot resolve.

But does this symptoms' database really contribute to a greater understanding of these problems? Like all health care professionals, Adlerians refer to the DSM-IV, but they have their own special way of searching for and understanding the root of a person's problem.

The Adlerian perspective

We've looked at Adler's approach to emotional disturbances in general. What did he have to say about mood disorders, a condition barely recognized in his lifetime?

Adler's original observations and teachings on all neurotic behavior strikingly prefigure our current thinking on these disorders. He recognized that most patients suffering from bipolar diseases experienced mood-swing tendencies long before they showed real symptoms. With remarkable prescience, Adler concluded that the bipolar mood swings had "bodily influences" that were components in the origins of the disorder. For Adler, someone born with a physical weakness may be vulnerable to the development of cycling moods. He also showed that the fate of the weak and "developmentally retarded" organ is varied. Inferiority or physical handicap can be overcome by physical and mental attributes compensated by the 'creative self'.

Adler recognized that patients who experience moods that swing back and forth continuously between extreme feelings of omnipotence and feelings of powerlessness lack faith in their own competence, and that their manic phases can be seen as maneuvers to deceive themselves and others. They use these feelings in making decisions rather than using common sense and logic, but they make contact with their reality in order to carry out their faulty logic. Having a grasp on reality, they are enormously sensitive, and even impatient. They know steps have to be taken to face their challenge, but they would rather not do so.

When Adler looked at the neurotic personality, he offered an essentially compassionate vision of a child overwhelmed, overburdened by circumstances and forced into a pattern of faulty logic. This type of logic may lead to parents pampering a child as the child unconsciously creates the circumstances to be spoiled. In other cases, there has been no pampering, but the parents have neglected the child and so allowed the child to choose this logic.

Almost all research in the last few decades supports Adler's view on neuroses and points to physiological factors in the origins of bipolar disorder. Adlerian thought has evolved today and there has been some research done linking specific forms of faulty logic and other common personality traits to the bipolar and the substance dependent person, traits and faulty logic that remain on an unconscious level for most.

Feeling becomes a more superior function of the mind than common sense or logic. Faulty logic like "I am different from the rest" or lofty goals like "I want to be the best in the world" drives the person to strive for impressive or even impossible feats to achieve. When he or she sees that this self-created goal cannot be achieved, anger and frustration sets in. A cyclical pattern emerges as the person then goes into a down cycle.

Adlerian research has shown that a high percentage of people with extreme mood swings are firstborn children and only children. Mania is a heightened attempt to achieve impressive feats; depression is the exhausted refusal to participate in life. These people are denied their achievement due to their depressive symptoms and low self-esteem, but they are still plagued by the strong manic desire to achieve and impress, and they continue to expend great energy to get what they want. They court the excitement in thinking about success and at the same time blame themselves for their failures. They think in extreme black or white, all or nothing terms. Balance and even-handedness are not in their portfolio of behaviors. They often retreat from their high-flying goals to attitudes of weakness and dependence on others.

Present day Adlerians see the following overlapping common traits in the people suffering from substance abuse with co-occuring moodcycling. To achieve their ambitious goal quickly and easily, people dependent on substances, use their drug(s) of choice self-destructively, medicating away their concerns and problems. There is a continuous, unfilled emptiness left by excruciating pain and suffering and guilt for what they are doing to themselves and others around them. They want to repair their courage and escape their responsibilities by using substances. They absolutely depend on others to carry out their life's responsibilities, but they are in denial that this is actually taking place.

II.
Creativity and Mood Swings

In the previous section, we established the link between self-created scripts from early childhood, neurosis and bipolar disorder. As a sufferer of mood swings, can you recognize any of these thoughts: "I have to be great"; or "If I am not great, then I am nothing"; "I'm on my way up in life conquering and overcoming or I'm on my way down — way down"? Have you ever thought of yourself as great as maybe another person you admire — maybe a world-famous talented individual? Perhaps these thoughts drive you at times with an almost demonic energy.

You are not alone. Many well-known gifted people have or had goals to achieve like someone they look up to. Often times, their "genius" was painful and difficult for them to maintain, or they did not feel their talents were adequately recognized. At these times, they would sink into the depths of melancholy.

Adler felt that highly talented individuals — people recognized for their "genius" — usually have contributed a great deal to the common welfare. Society has benefited from the genius of artists, musicians, writers, scientists, and world leaders that have taught us to how to see, think and feel differently, changing the world around us. He noted that their courage and leadership deserved our greatest dignity and respect.

Researchers have shown a relationship between genius and mood disorders — two enormously different possibilities — occurring at the same time in individuals. They have found the rates of manic-depression or major depression was 10 to 30 times more prevalent in world-famous artists than in the population at large. Musical geniuses such as Handel, Schumann, Berlioz, and Mahler had a high incidence of bipolar affective disorder or manic-depressive illness. In the 20th Century "New York School" of abstract artists, 50% of the artists were found to have a psychiatric disorder (predominantly a mood disorder) often compounded by alcohol abuse.

In yet another study, a large percentage of a sample of writers suffered some form of mood disorder. In this group, alcoholism was significantly more prevalent. Books and articles have been written about many in the entertainment business who are and were shown to have symptoms relating to these co-occurring disorders.

How did many in the gifted community share the fate of having a disordered personality with an unstable mood intermingled with a creative talent? The groundwork is laid in early childhood resulting in a "fundamental breakdown in inhibitory mechanisms" involved in seeing, thinking or doing things in a highly unusual way — out of the mainstream becomes the norm for these people. The "high" portion of the mood cycle (mild mania) can produce intense creative episodes.

Another common bipolar characteristic linked to creative people is an unusually intense focus. For example, the physicist, Sir Isaac Newton, was diagnosed as a manic-depressive, and he had long episodes of intense absorption day and night creating his scientific work. Being oversensitive to slights or challenges to their being tops in their field is yet another common feature. "Emotional reactivity" is a bipolar quality referring to how highly sensitive these individuals are to their environment and to their own internal processes.

We all have a spark of creativity in us. Everyday contributions made for the common good may lack in world-wide acclaim but, they are important in the cosmic scheme. Based on his years of experience with patients with mood swings, Dr. Ronald Fieve has proposed a "new and beneficial subtype" of manic depression called the Bipolar IIB category — not presently listed in the DSM-IV. These people use their "highs" to benefit society, self and family, having to deal with periodic depressions that get in the way.

By facing and challenging the agonies and difficulties that mood swings bring, by fighting the self-dissatisfaction and learning to work with and overcome the limitations they place on themselves, bipolar sufferers can maximize their chances of contributing to the world in a positive and constructive way.

5
Treating the Problem

There are hundreds of systems of psychotherapy, not to mention the many techniques that counselors draw on. People searching for help with moodcycling often wonder if the various health-care professionals — psychiatrists, other medical doctors, psychologists, psychotherapists, social workers, counselors — will diagnose and treat the condition in different ways. Some medical doctors and particularly psychiatrists can provide a form of talk therapy, and they are the only professionals who can prescribe psychotropic medication. But what is crucial is the connection between the therapist and the person seeking help. Without this connection, no further work can take place, and the therapist can always refer a client elsewhere based on the preliminary findings of the meeting.

Adlerian therapists reach out to the suffering person in a caring way. They offer hope and encouragement that patients can carry away and apply to their lives. Adler referred to this as a test of cooperation between equals. The therapist acts as an educator who allows the sufferer to develop a sense of universality, to feel equal to others rather than feel above or below them.

If, after reading this book, you decide to approach the Adlerian therapeutic community because you or someone you care for is suffering from a mood disorder and associated substance dependence, your therapist will encourage you to follow a number of paths, some of them simultaneously. Moodcycling and substance abuse cannot be treated in isolation. When psychiatric disorders and substance abuse disorders occur together, the likelihood of successful recovery from either is reduced unless both are treated simultaneously. It's important that you find a professional who is able to coordinate these various treatment paths. If your therapist enables you to realize you have these co-occuring problems and refers you to another resource such as a treatment center, you can always continue with the therapist you connected well with further along in your recovery.

Crisis intervention

The world of the dual-diagnosis patient is prone to calamity. The therapist must quickly resolve all immediate crises. The patient may be experiencing acute withdrawal symptoms after abruptly stopping use of alcohol and/or drugs. Before any other therapy can take place, they may require hospitalization to undergo a detoxification treatment. After a medical and psychiatric evaluation, doctors may stabilize the withdrawal symptoms with specific medications depending on what type of drug the person is withdrawing from. In any case, rest and proper nutrition is important at this time. After this critical period, the sufferer can be referred to a drug and alcohol rehabilitation program as an in-patient or an out-patient. At this stage, most patients do not do well with one-on-one therapy. The group setting, on the other hand, helps break through the denial processes.

At the same time, a therapist may encourage the patient to discontinue all contact with other users, and establish a connection to a substance dependence treatment program. Finding the patient a safe place to live may be a pressing issue and the therapist may have to make various arrangements with family members or friends. It may be necessary to contact the patient's employer or family members and obtain support to enter treatment. There also may be pressing legal issues to contend with.

Medication

A psychiatric assessment will be important even in early recovery. Many clinicians agree that medication is the cornerstone of treatment for the dual diagnosis of bipolar disorder and substance dependence. Abstaining suddenly from the drug(s) of choice — going "cold turkey"— may be life threatening and during this critical withdrawal stage in a hospital setting or detoxification program, tranquilizers and anticonvulsants may be life-saving. After the withdrawal phase, a doctor may prescribe antidepressants or mood stabilizers such as Prozac, Paxil or Lithium. Within a few weeks, these drugs can enable a recovering person to make clearer decisions about a treatment plan. Such medications help the suffering person control the manic phase of the mood swing, the phase that most often sabotages recovery. A list of effective agents appears in Appendix 3.

Alas, medication is not a cure in itself and comes with its own risks. If patients continue to use other substances while under medication, they may render the medication and treatment ineffective. And medication is only really effective in tandem with a form of cognitive behavioral therapy that identifies and deals with whatever may trigger a relapse, and with a talk therapy that deals with the motivation for change. It's this latter psychotherapy that Adlerians can provide.

Biopsychosocial recovery programs

These recovery programs for alcoholics and/or drug addicts, run by teams of experts, offer the best form of integrated treatment for the recovering dual-diagnosis patient. The team makes multiple assessments of the medical and psychiatric factors. It assesses the substance dependence and psychological state of the patient. It makes a life-style analysis of family and work situation, legal status and previous therapy. Specialized counselors and medical personnel will follow the early phase of the patient's recovery closely and ensure that he or she remains abstinent and takes the right doses of the right medication. Patients are usually asked to attend some type of in-patient or out-patient treatment program involving cognitive and behavioral modification in tandem with this stabilizing treatment of medication. Patients must learn what triggers their use of drugs and alcohol in order to achieve a stable abstinence, and learn how to prevent relapses. This is best achieved in group therapy, perhaps an Aftercare program for 6 to12 months after initial treatment, with individual therapy as an adjunct. It is in this setting that patients learn about the importance of the participation in the 12-step programs, the self-help format that has been in use for almost 70 years. It is well documented that people who attend these programs regularly have a lower relapse rate.

Understanding the "12 Steps and 12 Traditions" of these programs is essential for true recovery. (The Twelve Steps are described in more detail in Appendix 4). One of the biggest hurdles for the recovering person is the plunge into a healthy communal environment and these 12-step meetings offer just that. They are held in churches, synagogues and community centers seven days a week in cities and towns everywhere in the world. They provide recovering persons with invaluable support as they come to grips with denial, relapse, universality, and spirituality. Sponsors at the meetings are ready and willing to offer a hand in friendship. The newcomer and the sponsor in fact support one other as they climb the recovery ladder. Twelve-step members participate in discussion groups, groups that invite sharing and questions about the program. For the newcomers in the programs, help is only a telephone call away.

Statistics have shown that Alcoholics Anonymous has been more successful than any other therapy format in promoting the recovery from alcohol and drug addiction. Reputable treatment centers and counselors in the field insist on active participation in such programs.

Alternate therapies

After the first six months to a year of sobriety, the recovering person may want to search out alternate forms of therapy that would parallel the talking therapy and the group support as in the 12-step or aftercare programs. Other important changes in lifestyle include participation in an exercise program, learning progressive relaxation and breathing exercises, exploring changes in diet, and getting 8 hours of sleep per night.

Further alternate therapies known to help mind and body link include yoga and meditation. Bodywork therapies like therapeutic massage and shiatsu can be helpful, and "light" therapy has been known to counter the depressive symptoms of seasonal affective disorder. These bodywork therapies cannot take the place of, but act as an adjunct to the ongoing psychotherapy and Aftercare program.

Adlerian therapy and treatment

At a certain point, our patient is ready for the sort of thoughtful one-on-one therapy that can help him or her understand more of the underlying attitudes and styles-of-life that have given rise to — or at least exacerbated — the moodcycling condition that in turn can lead to substance dependence.

In Chapter 4, we looked at Adler's approach to therapy — the careful search for clues as to the meaning behind neurotic attitudes and behavior. Adler held to a holistic perspective whereby individuals are seen as indivisible, equal to more than the sum of their parts. For Adlerians, the symptoms show only part of the picture. They employ a variety of creative ways to connect with people, and motivate them through interventions that are tailored according to the nature and needs of the individual.

Besides looking at the biopsychosocial data and assessing it, the therapist helps patients identify thoughts that incorporate faulty logic and helps them learn to change negative thoughts into positive ones. Patient gradually acquires the conviction that personal mastery of decision-making can be attained through understanding — among other things — what role the addictive substance played in their lives. Drinking and drugging have a purpose. Adlerians therapists help their patients uncover the goals they created to avoid engaging in their life tasks.

Adlerians also describe four addictive personalities as shaped by their purposeful behavior. The "pleaser" needs to be liked and drinks or uses drugs to be accepted. "Controllers" create sideshows of using behavior away from life's tasks — ultimately ruling not only themselves, but family members as well. The "asserter" needs to feel superior and uses substances to feel more confident, assertive or aggressive. The "pleasure seeker" is looking for comfort and pleasure and uses alcohol or drugs to escape or mellow out. In all cases, these people silence the voice of the community around them spending their time with other alcoholics and addicts, avoiding non-using family and friends. Social interest fades and the five life tasks that Adlerians describe progressively weaken.

The therapist seeks to reverse this process by strengthening these areas and strives to inculcate what Raymond Corsini calls the *"four R's"*: to treat others and self with respect, to learn to carry out responsibilities, to be responsive in a positive way, and to learn to be resourceful. The therapist eases the patient into engagement with each of these life tasks through encouragement, continually reminding the patient of his or her choices in the treatment. As difficult a process as this may be, Adlerian therapists have found that the further patients progress in their life tasks, the greater their chances of long-term recovery. Let's looks again at each of the life tasks and see how they play out in the case of a dual-diagnosis patient.

The life task of the self. A big task for recovering patients is to overcome their denial that they have a problem with mood swings and substance use. They must develop this awareness before any other changes can take place but, with the admission that there is a problem, the door swings open to change. Patients may alter their diet, start an exercise program, or look at a new hobby or recreation. Later in the treatment, they may become more aware of how faulty thinking got them into trouble and learn more logical ways of thinking — heavily accented with common sense — as they learn to understand those factors that triggered swings in mood and triggered drug use.

The life task of social relationships (friendship and / or community). Often, the only friends patients have are drinking or drug-using companions. We have already seen how the therapist will encourage a patient's involvement in group therapies such as the 12-step programs and rehabilitation programs. It is sometimes better to start the socialization process with strangers who are afflicted in a similar way, before reaching out to known friends and relatives who have already been affected by the affliction.

The life task of school and/or work. As you may already know, these disorders are extremely punishing on work and career. The therapist and the patient may decide to call in teachers, school counselors, human resources personnel, fellow employees and/or employers. This can be a valuable part of treatment if the patient is having difficulty readjusting to these environments. As patients learn to accept responsibility for their recovery, they can start looking at how their faulty belief systems have affected their performance at work or school and begin to develop new goals in these areas. Sometimes, if the job environment is a major stressor, a recovering person decides to change their area of study or career. A career counselor may help.

The life task of intimacy (love, marriage and parenting). Although, at the onset of therapy, the therapist may declare a "time out" from those closest to the patient, he or she must learn again to reach out to the family and understand the family members' positive intention. They may serve as the best support in the long run.

A special case arises when both marital partners live together and are addicted to substances. Unless both go in for separate treatment and go to separate group therapies and meetings, the likelihood for relapse is great. It is difficult but not impossible for both partners to recover and stay together if both agree to learn effective coping strategies with the help of a therapist in face-to-face discussions.

The life task of the spiritual. The therapist's work, sometimes in conjunction with a 12-step program, can help a recovering person understand more about their relationship with the cosmos, with a Higher Power, with life itself. Patients may be helped to understand that they are not the center of the universe. The therapist or the 12-step program is not there to impose any religious belief whatsoever, but patients may nonetheless establish or reestablish a connection with their own spirituality through a personal path or as part of organized religious groups in the community.

Through developing the motivation and skills to meet the life tasks, the recovering person can let go of the preoccupation with self, evolve socially, and experience a profound sense of belonging and a genuine interest in the welfare of others.

6
Helping Those Who Care

In this section, we'll address those people who are closest to dual-diagnosis patients. These are usually their parents or spouses, and sometimes their grandparents, their siblings or even their children. But it can be others too — close friends, lovers, co-workers, employers and employees — in fact anyone who cares and whose life may be bound up with the afflicted person. And if you, reader, are the patient, don't skip this chapter. You're probably already aware of the burden this illness places upon the people around you and you may find something here useful to yourself.

At this point, you might well be thinking to yourself, "All right. That's enough about why my daughter is the way she is. I know she's had it rough in some ways, but so have a lot of people." Or you might think, "Sure, sure. But what's wrong with my husband showing a little strength of character? Why is it *me* who has to be the responsible one, the self-disciplined one? It's *his* problem we're talking about." Or perhaps, "Frankly, I'm worn out. It's one crisis after another and all because of *his* weakness."

There are few families of dual diagnosis patients that aren't harboring real feelings of hurt, frustration and impatience.

Denial

At first, particularly if the person is a member of your family, as is usually the case, you may understandably try to deny that there is a problem. You try to keep everything normal. You might even manage to sustain this denial for a long period — years perhaps. Let's assume it's your son, for example, whose mood swings over a period of years have now indisputably led to a disabling drug addiction. This is a nightmare for any family. You want to accept his explanations — they're rationalizations of course — as true. The last thing you want is some lurid drug scandal providing grist for the local gossip mill. You cover for him when you can and tell yourself it's only fair to give the young man the benefit of the doubt. But as he persists, pushing the envelope ever and ever harder, your efforts at maintaining a façade of normalcy are less successful. At one point, you consider some of your history as a family and decide that the whole thing is your fault — you and your spouse. You may not be able sustain this perspective indefinitely though, because it's often a fiction, a merciful fiction you've worked up to spare yourself the truth: your son's behavior is stubborn and intractable. Maybe your marriage is falling apart. You withdraw further from your old social circle. It's too painful to hear your friends describe their children's glowing accomplishments. They're merciless, you feel. They're watching you. Then one day, you get a call from your son's employer.

Admission and Enabling

Gradually you come to accept that your son's behavior and drug use is abnormal. But there's nothing easy about this stage either. You thought you had some control of the affairs of your household, or at least that there was nothing serious to control. Now you have to admit that, just when you'd most like to exert control, you cannot. Nothing you do works. You try everything. You try to prevent him gaining access to the extra money for drugs, you try to keep him out of trouble, and you try at least to limit his intake of illicit chemicals. You try to protect him, in other words and this protecting behavior is known an "enabling".

We can hear the alarm bells at this point. It's the normal reaction. "Enabling?" you say, "Then I am to blame. I'm to blame for helping him to continue like this, destroying himself!"

At this point, we're going to draw a fine line. A troubling condition has afflicted this person you love, but its root causes are not known to you, or to your loved one. Alfred Adler's theories of personality allow for both nature and nurture — and probably both — as possible causes. Substance dependence is, in the end, a family illness — a mutual destruction pattern psychologists call codependence. The bottom line is: you have a problem because your loved one has a problem.

It is possible, of course, if you are a parent of the patient, that you actually contributed to your child's condition through some action of gross irresponsibility such as neglect or abuse. Or perhaps, as parent or spouse, you have provided a tainted example such as alcoholism or drug abuse. If any of these circumstances should be the case, then you too are a sufferer and you too need help.

But most often this is not the case. Each family member needs to search out his or her own healing process. Most often, your responsibility, especially as a parent or spouse, lies in the present: to help change your loved one's behavior and help them to recovery.

Helping, not Enabling

Let's imagine that you have a wife whose history of mood swings has culminated in full-blown bipolar disorder and this, you've finally come to recognize, is complicated by alcoholism. You have done everything possible to obtain professional help for the bipolar condition, but the alcoholism seems to render your efforts useless. Now what? Certainly, your wife must take ultimate responsibility for her life if she is going to get better.

You face a challenge that is much like hers. You must identify all your own behaviors and reactions that have made it even more difficult for her to recover than it would otherwise be. Your wife may have spent years convincing herself and you that she was in control of her mood disorder and her drinking. You knew better at some level, but allowed yourself to believe her. You'd call work for her and explain that she was home with another cold when in fact she was sleeping off a hangover. You locked the liquor cabinet and hid the car keys, ran to the bank to cover unexpected overdrafts and maxed-out credit cards. You tidied up ashtrays and washed out glasses before leaving for work in the morning. When all failed, you blamed yourself; you'd been too hard on her; you should never have pressured her.

Now, whoever your loved one may be, and whoever you may be, all this must change. Now you must surrender to the truth. You simply cannot control this disorder no matter what you do. What then?

First, you must re-acquaint yourself with your own dignity. You've given up a sizable portion of self-esteem in order to maintain the fiction of your loved one's normalcy. You're worth more than that and so are the other family members who were neglected or abused in the course of this illness. Your own personal growth is also a valid goal. Taking control of your life is also an imperative. If you feel you are having difficulty doing this alone, remember that you are not alone. There are support groups for you, just as there are for patients.

The Al-Anon and Alateen family groups, Co-Anon and Nar-Anon, and Adult Children of Alcoholics (ACOA) are so-called co-dependency groups that can be found in the Yellow Pages of your telephone directory, and on the Internet. Or you may decide at this stage to see a psychotherapist about your family problem. Or you may decide to set up a "family intervention" that employs a person specialized in confronting patients with their behavior. Such strategies may entail inviting caring friends or family to attend in an effort to convince the patient to get help. It's possible, as you can see, that the search for your own dignity and happiness may in this way lead directly to real help for the person who is actually sick.

Second, you and others may have to put some distance between yourselves and the patient. True, if you're not right there, you won't be able to prevent the ensuing free-fall, but that's the point: free-fall is what's required. Your poor wife — or husband, child or friend — must be allowed to reach their bottom, the point when they are finally shocked by their car accident, their own violence, or some other extreme of self-disgrace, and join others in the realization that things cannot go on like this. Now, third, the road lies open to positive actions by which you can play a real role in the psychological and physical salvation of this person you love.

Doing Good

Of course you will attempt to obtain professional help for your child, spouse or friend. Their bipolar condition is a serious matter that is not in their direct control. But present-day integrated therapies and medications have proven a powerful ally in diminishing the distressing symptoms and harmful effects of this disorder.

Once your dual-diagnosis person you care for is in treatment, you'll need to look at the question of "limit setting", if you already have not addressed these issues. If your recovering alcoholic son lives with you, you might want to review what exactly you would require from him that would allow you to be less anxious. A curfew may be appropriate is some cases. If he wants to go out at night, for example, you may both agree that he must tell you where he is going and leave a telephone number with you. That, after all, is when a lot of the trouble begins, isn't it? When he is out at night and wanders over to a bar?

Earlier, we saw how difficult treatment for dual disorders can be. Abstinence can play a crucial role in this treatment and family members can be profoundly supportive and encouraging by deciding to create a drug-free home environment, or at family get-togethers if the patient does not live with family members. Conversely, when the patient doesn't live with the family, the family can decide how often they want to get together and whether they really want to see these loved ones when they are under the influence.

Now is the time to be honest about what is happening in your family. Share information with other family members. Do whatever you can to increase your communications and understand how they are feeling. Family secrets only help to increase the denial that there is a problem.

Take this opportunity to learn as much as you can about these disorders and how they affect all family members. "I'm not the one with the problem," you say, "and I still have to work so hard at it!" In a sense you're right, of course, but these afflictions can seriously affect the health of those closest to the patient and your knowledge can be an important part of your own protection. Again, the so-called 12 steps of non-profit fellowship programs like Al-Anon and Alateen may prove valuable aids for family and friends. A great deal of literature is available on the 12 steps for co-dependents, and some suggestions are listed in the Bibliography.

If you are of a religious nature, now may be the time to get in touch with your spirituality and develop it further. For many families, the belief in a Higher Power provides support and comfort while opening the way to a more satisfying life.

When at last your loved one enters treatment, be as open as you feel you can to participation in their therapy or treatment program. Family therapy has proved effective in reaching real understanding of family dynamics, in promoting new coping skills, and in improving communication skills. It's a powerful experience to sit in a group therapy session with other family members who are suffering in the same way.

You'll discover how much you have in common. Some of the best results achieved in the recovery of dual-diagnosis patients have resulted when family dynamics were changed and communication between family members became more open and honest.

Lastly, you should know that there are others even more innocent than yourself. No one is left untouched and children in the household are easily affected by these events. Turn your attention to them if they are there, and see how these disorders in their siblings or parent have affected this other members of the family. They may often believe themselves to be at fault for all the trouble in the family. They may either react by being super good or act out their insecure feelings through rebellious and naughty behavior. Take the time to explain to children that the patient is ill and not linked in any way to themselves. There are several good books for children at different age levels that help them understand what is happening in the family. See the Bibliography for a short reading list.

7
A Few Thoughts about Drugs

You may feel you already hear enough about drugs — on television, in the newspapers and from anything associated with teenagers. As a dual-diagnosis patient or as someone close to such a person, you may rightly feel you've had plenty of personal exposure. But the subject of drugs is not a static one – it's constantly evolving, not only with the invention of new substances, but with the discovery that some very ordinary — indeed ubiquitous — substances are by themselves drugs.

Our interest in these small amounts of chemical that can produce big changes in our minds and our bodies transcends historical periods and specific cultures. And probably no category of drugs piques our curiosity more than the so-called psychoactive drugs — the drugs that affect our minds, our perceptions, our thinking, our moods. There would seem to be a very human yearning to change our consciousness, to experience a higher state, a feeling of euphoria and lightness. Even as children, we appear to express that aspiration — we rock, we spin, we hyperventilate, and we tickle one another into altered states.

As adults, we may resort to chemicals in an effort to change our everyday consciousness. Psychedelic drugs transform our perceptions. Mood-altering drugs help us deal with the mental presets that make us feel uncomfortable or cause us to react badly to the world around us. Stimulants excite us. Tranquillizers relax us.

It is a small wonder that psychoactive drugs are the most abused drugs known even today and small wonder that we must maintain a good relationship with these drugs. Awareness and education are important tools, since the consequences of a bad relationship with drugs are bad indeed. We can lose control of our use of the drug so that we require more and more to achieve the effect we originally wanted. Eventually, we may hardly experience that effect at all, but experience instead serious and unwanted side effects that impair our health and behavior. As the drug begins to control us rather than the other way around, we may start to have problems at work, at school, with our family and with our friends. And as you may know too well, people with a mood-swing disorder are vulnerable to bad relationship with drugs. They and their loved ones need to be on heightened alert when using them.

Many drugs are illegal and some — heroin is an example — might even be said to be taboo. But our society is replete with substances that are neither illegal nor taboo but that in many respects act like drugs. Because they are easily available, some of us may us may slip into using them indiscriminately with little thought to the consequences.

Sugar. Sugar is a prime ingredient in countless food products. In its refined form — the form in which we most often encounter it — it is a white crystalline substance that occurs naturally in fruit, vegetables and dairy products. It has no smell but a direct and intensely attractive taste — no wonder, since our bodies have been conditioned by countless generations of evolution to respond to this most concentrated carbohydrate, a precious source of energy when such sources were hard to come by. Processed sugar is so concentrated a food, so easily absorbed, that not only does it have a strong energy-boosting effect on our bodies it sets off a chain reaction that reaches our brains by causing a rise in our blood-insulin levels that leads in turn to a rise in the serotonin levels in our brains. Serotonin is a mood elevator. Voila! We feel better and perhaps perform better. Not surprisingly then, sugar has the potential to be psychologically habit-forming, and perhaps physically too. That's why it qualifies as an invisible drug.

People in a good relationship with sugar are able to control their use of these appealing little crystals. Just as with other drugs, a good relationship means we understand it, control our pattern of use, can separate from it easily and experience few side effects. A bad relationship with sugar develops when we consume large and frequent amounts, cannot do without it, and perhaps start to experience adverse changes to our metabolism and mood.

If we persist in eating and drinking too much sugar, our elevated serotonin levels begin to fall and eventually fall below normal. Voila! We're depressed! This lack of brain serotonin leads to varying degrees of depression. If we don't know better, we rush off to eat more sugar in an effort to keep our mood up. Meanwhile, our bodies are responding to all this sugar by producing massive amounts of insulin to counter the high blood-sugar levels. Insulin depresses mood and, although the effects of sugar are short-lived, insulin's actions are longer-lived. The overall result can be a further trigger to depression and lethargy. This may be the route to a physiological addiction to sugar. And we haven't even considered the other side effects: the damage to our teeth and such life-threatening consequences as obesity and diabetes.

For those already contending with mood-swing propensities, sugar's potential to push these swings higher and lower will be obvious.

Caffeine. Coffee was introduced into Europe from Africa 1000 years ago. Later, tea and cocoa found their way into our Western diet. Perhaps the world's most widely used stimulant, caffeine, a bitter crystalline substance and a member of the xanthine family is found in tea (27mg per cup) and coffee (66 to 112 mg per cup). Chocolate, cocoa and cocoa butter are derived from the cocoa bean and also contain caffeine, and the closely-related xanthine, theobromine. A chocolate bar can contain 20mg caffeine. More recently, cola drinks came along to offer us caffeine (35mg per can) derived from the kola nut. Caffeine is also found in non-prescription pain-relievers, cold remedies and stimulant mixtures.

Short-term physical effects of caffeine include an increase in the following: metabolic rate, body temperature, blood pressure, and urination. Caffeine stimulates the secretion of stomach acid and decreases the appetite. Caffeine products shorten the sleep cycle, can lead to hand tremors and impairment of fine coordination of movement. Large doses of caffeine produce nervousness, headache, and possibly delirium.

Regular use of more than 8 cups of coffee per day (600mg caffeine) can cause chronic insomnia, persistent stomach upset, anxiety and depression. Heavy caffeine use in pregnancy has been linked to birth defects.

These potentially habit-forming drinks are everywhere but much depends on what kind of relationship we have with them. Those already engaged in a battle with moodcycling disorders, however, might at least consider that the American Psychiatric Association is contemplating adding "Caffeine Dependence Syndrome" to its next DSM. This syndrome, if it comes, will describe those who have failed to establish a good relationship with caffeine products. In other words, a negative relationship with caffeine can lead to a form of physical dependence; and withdrawal from caffeine results in fatigue, irritability, and severe headaches.

Nicotine. For many people, the day starts with a nice cup of coffee or tea, sweetened perhaps with sugar, and a cigarette. Without them, they may not be able to start the day without real distress. When the smoke of the dry, shredded leaves of the tobacco plant is inhaled deeply into the lungs, the nicotine it contains reaches the brain within a few seconds. This potent, short-acting stimulant is the most psychoactive (though not necessarily the most dangerous) of the almost 4000 chemicals that may be present in or added to cigarette tobacco.

Nicotine is appealing to a young person entering the teenage years and beginning to experiment with adult behaviors. The impact of adult realities and the loss of childhood's rosy perspective can be stressful and even depressing. Nicotine is a quick, accessible way to alter these down moods and it may for some kids be the "gateway" drug preceding the recreational use of alcohol, marijuana, cocaine, or other drugs. Though they may pay lip service to medical warnings, not many young smokers are aware that they have entered a relationship with one of the most dangerous and addicting drugs known.

Nicotine is able to produce a physical and psychological dependence that is equivalent to that produced by heroin, which enjoys a reputation as the most addictive drug. Of those who decide to quit smoking tobacco, 80% will return to its use within four years. The relapse rate can be somewhat reduced with nicotine replacement therapy — like the nicotine patch or gum. It's arguable that more people are addicted to tobacco than any other drug.

The short-term physiological effects of nicotine are similar to those of caffeine: increased blood pressure and heart rate, drop in skin temperature, increased breathing, shortened sleep and decreased appetite.

The long-term effects are dramatically different: each cigarette cuts about five minutes from the smoker's lifespan. By 65, smokers have a rate of death three times higher than non-smokers. By 75, they are twice as likely to die. Accumulation of the tar by-products of burning cigarettes leads to diseases like chronic bronchitis, emphysema, cardiovascular disease, and cancer of the lungs, mouth, and throat. Carbon monoxide, a gas present in tobacco smoke, weakens the heart, the lungs, the cardiovascular system. Smoking causes stomach ulcers, the narrowing of blood vessels and a decrease in vitamin C levels. Smoking cigarettes while pregnant can irreparably damage the developing fetus and have a detrimental effect on the child's growth and intellectual development. The health of those living with the smoker may suffer from the effects of passively inhaling the toxic smoke.

Alcohol. Alcohol, a by-product of the action of yeast on sugar, is a profoundly psychoactive drug. It is often observed that, were it to be invented today, it would never be made legal.

For many people, the moderate use of alcohol is pleasant, relaxing and even medicinal. There is evidence that up to two standard drinks a day may have a number of beneficial effects for the body. Alcohol doesn't affect everyone in the same way. Some people have a high tolerance for the drug, and others are made physically sick by ingesting a comparatively small amount. This everyday observation points to what may be a genetic factor in alcoholism, the habitual and uncontrolled use of alcohol.

Teenagers in our culture drink alcohol as part of the rites of passage into the adult world. Apart from the immediate psychological effects, drinking alcohol — like smoking tobacco — imparts adult status because it is adult behavior. But because many teens experience a sense of personal failure, live amidst family chaos, or have some difficulty fitting in with their peers, they may find seductive alcohol's ability to relieve anxiety, and numb out feelings of sadness, grief and depression. Not surprisingly, these teenagers are at risk to become problems drinkers.

One standard drink (12 ounces of 5% beer, 5 ounces of 14% wine or 1.5 ounces of 80-proof liquor) contains 13.6 grams of absolute alcohol. The liver, however, can only process 8 to 12 grams of alcohol per hour. When blood alcohol levels are 0.05% and above, the drinker may experience a feeling of euphoria and a release of inhibitions, with flushing of the face and some drowsiness. But as the blood alcohol increases, there is an escalating impairment of judgment and vision, a loss of concentration and slowed reaction time. Excessive drinking leads to slurred speech, staggering and double vision. A person is very drunk when the blood-alcohol level reaches 0.2%, with staggering, emotional instability, and violent reactions. Shakiness, nausea, vomiting and headaches may continue into the "hangover" period 8 to 12 hours later, when all euphoria is well and truly gone.

The catastrophic effects of drinking and driving are of ever growing concern to society as a whole. When the blood-alcohol level reaches 0.1%, drivers are legally classified as drunk and most drivers are significantly impaired. They are six times more likely to be involved in a car crash than sober drivers. Drinking three or four per hour produces this result. With a blood-alcohol level of 0.2%, the risk of a crash is 100 times more likely.

Twenty to thirty percent of all accidents have been directly linked to alcohol consumption. These include fires, suicide attempts, work-related and recreational accidents, college failures and pedestrians killed on the road. Seventy percent of all drowning and physical assaults are alcohol-related, including spousal violence. Chronic heavy use results in disruptions in the alcoholic's social, family and working life.

However benign it may be in moderation, alcohol is a highly destructive substance when abused. An obvious symptom of alcohol abuse is increased tolerance over a period of time. For the desired psychological effect of relief, the immoderate drinker must drink increasingly large amounts of alcohol over time. As the dependence for alcohol develops, the drinker may develop withdrawal symptoms such as jumpiness, sweating, poor appetite, and sleeplessness when the drinking stops. Severe withdrawal may entail tremors, hallucinations, and death.

Abuse of alcohol over a long period of time has its physiological consequences as well. These include loss of memory and blackouts, and the destruction of brain cells leading to what is known as "water on the brain". Alcohol can trigger bleeding and ulcers in the stomach and intestines, and is linked to cancer in these organs. The liver of an alcoholic suffers more than any other organ. The excess calories are stored in the liver as fat and the "fatty liver" is one of the earliest sign of alcoholism. The fat eventually destroys the liver tissue and the result is a fatal disease, cirrhosis. The heart muscle deteriorates with chronic excessive use of alcohol. The immune system is weakened, leading to a growing vulnerability to bacterial and viral infections. Men become impotent, and women's menstrual cycles become irregular. Drinking alcohol during pregnancy may trigger the development of birth defects in children. Because alcohol's high caloric content displaces key nutrients, its abuse leads readily to malnutrition.

Cannabis. The leaves and oil of the cannabis plant has for centuries been the recreational drug of preference in North Africa and parts of the Middle East. Its use in North America appears to have spread, especially after the middle of the twentieth century. Today marijuana and related cannabis products such as the more potent hashish, made from the plant's resin, follow closely on the heels of tobacco smoking and alcohol consumption as the most popular drugs. The active ingredient is tetrahydrocannabinol (THC).

Marijuana use is still considered illegal in the United States, although laws governing its possession vary widely in Europe. Some countries have recently moved to decriminalize simple possession and legalized the use of marijuana to ameliorate the symptoms of multiple sclerosis, to reduce fluid pressure in cases of glaucoma, and to ease the nausea associated with chemotherapy. There is continuing controversy over the liberalization of cannabis laws.

Polysubstance Abuse. The use of a variety drugs on a regular basis is more common today than previously. Users have easy access to many drugs and when drugs are combined, the effects can be unexpected and unwanted. Seventy percent of all visits to emergency rooms in Toronto, Canada are due to drug combinations.

When depressant drugs are combined — for example when alcohol is combined with sleeping pills or tranquilizers — their separate depressant effects are intensified. Respiratory depression is a particularly serious consequence, which, if not treated properly, can lead to coma and death.

Most young people want to flee what they see as restrictive home environments to be with their peer group. Since the early 1990s, rave parties have been a seductive, supposedly safe environment: a return for one night to the carefree existence of childhood. Raves — if you should be somehow unfamiliar with them — are essentially dusk-to-dawn dances in a big space such as a warehouse, with intense electronic music and a large number of young people. Many different drugs are available at raves, including ecstasy, GHB (gamma hydroxybutyrate), Rohypnol, ketamine, rhodies, marijuana, LSD (lysergic acid diethylamide), amphetamines, alcohol, caffeine and nitrous oxide. Heroin and cocaine have not found favor at raves.

Drugs available on the street or at raves are of uncertain doses and quality. They are prepared by people who are dealing illegally and unaccountably. There products cannot be trusted. Marijuana can be contaminated with substances like PCP (phenylcyclidine) or paraquat, a poisonous herbicide. Magic mushrooms can be sprayed with PCP or LSD. Ecstasy, already suspected of causing brain damage, can be misformulated. It is impossible to know the strength or true contents of any pill without having it tested in the laboratory.

Needless to say, those taking prescribed psychoactive medications such as anti-depressants are at particular risk of sabotaging their treatment by using recreational drugs including alcohol.

Appendix 5 lists short-term and long-term effects of all categories of mind-altering drugs. Other resources for information about psychoactive drugs are listed in the Bibliography.

8
Defeating the Dread of Change

You may well have discovered — and even become attached to — some aspects of your bipolar or addicted life style. You may well enjoy the pleasures of high intelligence that sometimes accompanies the condition — or unusual sensitivity or artistic creativity. Yet you've always had to admit that with the positive has come the negative, and in the end, the wild swings are exhausting and debilitating. The long journey to recovery lies ahead.

When we think about taking a journey — even a journey to a country of clean air and endless vistas — we can feel apprehensive. And if you're a person suffering from a mood-swing disorder and perhaps some sort of substance dependence, the metaphorical journey to wellness we've described in this book might inspire similar apprehension. It's natural to fear the disruption of a pattern we've come to know and think of as our own.

Some tasks are dauntingly difficult to undertake alone, but these mood and substance problems are doubly difficult because they impair some aspects of your rational thinking and even take the edge off your common sense. You'll need a strong desire to get better and we are not going to pretend it will be easy. But please, this is not a journey to be undertaken alone. Sooner or later, all of us mortals need someone to hold our hand.

The bad news, as you've probably already learned, is that these conditions can be chronic and real stability may entail a lifetime of vigilance. The good news is that medication and psychotherapy actually do the job.

Virtually everyone who works with dual-diagnosis patients agrees that modern medications are usually effective in bringing about a better balance in the brain chemistry responsible for ordering mood. But the long-term patterns associated with mood disorders may require more than balanced brain chemistry. Many studies now support what Adlerian and other psychotherapists have long believed — for those who are willing, those who put recovery first, and those who want to gain as much knowledge as they can about their own patterns of thought and behavior, severe mood swings can be substantially reduced or sometimes entirely controlled.

A loving relative or close friend may be the point of leverage that will help you break the cycle. You may want to approach your parent, your spouse, your sibling or your best friend to tell them that you now realize that you're suffering from severe mood swings and/or addiction, and need their help. Together you can search for a doctor, a psychotherapist or a self-help group to get you started. And although a supportive family is a big plus, many people who have not enjoyed this advantage have found their way to help and achieved fulfilling and productive lives. In the end, after all, only you can really take care of you. *You* best know your own limitations, quirks and realistic needs.

Perhaps you're uncomfortable going to a family member. In this case, reach out to the helping profession on your own. Begin by educating yourself, as you're already doing by reading this book. You might discreetly ask friends or maybe consult the human resources department at work. The Yellow Pages usually list the phone numbers for hot-lines you can call about mental disorders, addiction and alcoholism. Can you trust an absolute stranger to listen to your innermost fears and possibly "crazy" thoughts? It takes courage, yes, but really, what is the alternative? Living your life on an emotional roller coaster that carries you further and further from the joys life has to offer?

You pick a therapist, and pluck up the courage to go once, then come out of the office sweating and filled with anger. "This isn't for me!" you say. "There must be an easier way!" Or, "Why medication?" Or — this is a common reaction — "Jeez, I didn't like *her*." A rapport can fail to develop between you and a therapist for any number of reasons, but make sure you're not sabotaging your treatment plan by blaming a rough start on the other person. Push yourself to revisit the offending professional and discuss your unfavorable reaction. Or try someone else— it's your prerogative. The important thing is to take an active part in selecting a therapist who feels right for you. It *must* be someone you trust.

You might seek out the guidance of your physician. He or she may recommend that you get a psychiatric assessment. Your medical advisor may recommend an antidepressant or other medication in tandem with psychotherapy. Some patients worry that they may become addicted to this new medication — not surprising, perhaps, given their sometimes harrowing histories with other drugs. But of course these new medications simply regulate the physical side of illness and do *not* produce a physical addiction. They can only work, though, for people who are totally committed to staying on the medication regime *and* they require several weeks to begin effectively balancing mood.

Today there are many medications to choose from. A good doctor may explore the options until one emerges that's right for you. You might grow apprehensive and think you're someone's guinea pig, but this trial and error is routine. Persevere with your doctor until you find the right prescription and dosage.

If you're the type of person who just can't see herself or himself taking pills on a regular basis over a long period of time, seeing a psychologist or psychotherapist — a good idea for any bipolar or dual-diagnosis patient — becomes an imperative. The goal of "talking" therapy such as that practiced by Adlerians is to break the cycle of mood swings and to learn a new way of living — not an easy task for anyone, but a task with great rewards.

You'll need to become committed to this new idea of seeking and receiving help on a regular basis. You'll find excuses not to go, perhaps, but the choice is between living fully and living with irrational thoughts, fears, insecurities and fantasies that get you into trouble and paralyze your life.

A therapist can help you get better by detecting when you're struggling or resisting. He or she will assist you up the steep rises and, although you may still have to do a lot of climbing alone, show you where the path may be easier.

We've had a chance to look at some of the characteristics of a person suffering from these co-occuring disorders. Here's another way to think about the condition: damaging thoughts fly by uncaught. If we're going to effect a recovery, we have to become acutely aware of as many of these thoughts as possible, since each leads to a potentially harmful reaction of mind and body. We must learn to catch these negative thoughts before they get a chance to do damage — catch them, assess them and change them. As a net for these thoughts, we can begin to ask ourselves some questions.

You may ask the question, "Is this the type of thought I have had as a child growing up in my family?" For example, maybe you are thinking: "See, I am a failure again!" The reaction to this thought might be: "Well, I'll show you!" followed by a manic spin into hyperactivity. Or, at another point in the cycle, you may think, "So true. I'm hopeless," and then you withdraw into isolation and depression.

"Is this thought making me uncomfortable right now?" you ask. Maybe your heart is racing, your muscles are tense, and you are hardly breathing.

If the answers to these questions are "yes", there's a further question. Asked and answered, it has the ability to take us to a better place. The question is: "What can I do or think differently that will make me more comfortable based on my present reality?" Can you think of something positive you have achieved in the past twenty-four hours? You can take a deep breath, catch yourself, stretch, and think of ways to change the thought, so you can start to reverse the discomfort and relax.

As we learn to spot and catch these thoughts, we can pose quite different questions. "Do I want to continue this thought? It leaves me feeling like I'm still the kid at home — still doing this and that for Mom and Dad. Maybe I can think or do something else. After all, I'm an adult and this is a *new* reality. Yes, I'm an adult. Then what can I think differently? What can I do differently?" From these reflections, it's a short leap to: "Hey! I'm twenty-three! I've got a new reality. I can take control of my life *today*. What small new thought can I think to take me out of this slump — or this high?" And then: "Today — right now — I can make a plan and I can carry out that plan. I can end up feeling comfortable with myself, not falling into my usual tail-spin, or my usual soaring over the moon and away!"

Can we be vigilant about every thought? In a world of instant fixes where everyone is impatient when something takes too much effort, it may not be easy. It may be a lot like playing the piano — hours of practice every day to get it right. But what an achievement!

That's the crux. How much are you willing to extend yourself to really get better? It may take a lot of practice, with many mistakes over a long period of time before you begin to feel you've really made the breakthrough. In the meantime, falling apart because you made a mistake is no option at all. You're not hurting anyone else by learning. And if you do feel you've hurt someone else, you'll take responsibility and describe and explain your error.

You and your doctor have been successful in choosing a medication that has helped you balance out. You have a trusting relationship with your therapist and you're becoming more aware of your style of life and where the weak links are in the dynamics with your family members, with yourself and with your life tasks. You've been monitoring your mood swings and your daily activity.

Then you hit a roadblock. For no apparent reason, you stop looking forward to your visits to the therapist. You can sense the old patterns are re-emerging. You begin to make mistakes. "I can't do it after all!" you despair, "I can't keep control!"

This is a normal part of the therapeutic process. It's impossible to progress as though you were marching to the steady beat of a drum. Maybe you've exhausted yourself. Maybe you're scared — and no one likes to think of themselves as scared.

But we're talking here about fear of change, not cowardice. Rationally, our minds start to accept the new ways of thinking and behaving, but emotionally we reject these new ways. After years of practice, the old ways are more comfortable. A new pair of shoes looks beautiful in the store and seems so right. You leave them in the box until you put them on for a special occasion. Ouch. In fact, they hurt when you've gone just a block or two. It takes some walking time to work out the kinks. That's how it is with change. You need time to muster up the courage to practice newer ways of thinking, ways that are finally more comfortable than the old ones and are based on your present-day realities. The option is going back to being that kid again, growing up in your family of origin, wearing those tired old shoes.

With encouragement from your support network, you decide instead to start over again. Even in the middle of a relapse, the good news is that now you're aware of what you're doing. Forgive yourself quickly — the more time goes by, the longer it will take to turn around again. Back to Square One, but this time, Square One is not the first square. You've been through this before and it's going to be easier to regroup and rethink this time. This time you have some tools under your belt, and a support system in place, and caring people to reach out to. You may have to go back to that Square One many times. Mistakes are excellent teachers for people willing to rectify them.

It's important to know that you are not alone in your struggles with yourself. Every human being who has ever lived has struggled in some way. Those that can sustain hope and motivate themselves and reach out to people who can inspire them, can achieve a life that is truly worth living. If that life is spotted with difficulty here and there, the difficulty is surmountable as we find new ways to change and help ourselves. We need to learn to be our own very best friend first.

Changing is like learning to walk all over again, but in a less crippled way. The good news is that you have learned to walk properly once, so you can relearn much faster each time you err. Meanwhile, never ever give up on yourself or the process called change. You're worth it. We all have great potential in this wonderful cosmos!

Appendix I: The DSM-IV on Bipolar Disorder

Adler's approach was essentially different from medically-based psychological systems that grew up after Freud, but there are some important similarities between his way of assessing patients and a diagnosis based on the Diagnostic and Statistical Manual of Mental Disorders (the DSM-IV), psychiatry's standard reference book. The American Psychiatric Association first issued this manual in 1952. It classified psychopathological symptoms in the Diagnostic and Statistical Manual of Mental Disorders (DSM-1). There have been five major revisions of this manual in the last 50 years. It has been the mainstay of most North American clinicians who have had their training according to the medical disease model. The manual is a useful catalogue, but makes no attempt to explain the underlying causes of behavioral dysfunction. Both the Adlerian approach and the DSM-IV, however, base their diagnoses on overall evaluations of a patient's biological, psychological and social systems. The DSM-IV breaks down Bipolar Disorder into three related disorders and establishes the current terminology:

Bipolar I Disorder: "Characterized by the occurrence of one or more Manic Episodes or Mixed Episodes. Often individuals have also had one or more Major Depressive Episodes." The mania appears to be more predominant in Bipolar I patients, and is destructive unless treated. In between these episodes, the person has tremendous energy (p. 350-351).

Bipolar II Disorder: "Characterized by the occurrence of one or more Major Depressive Episodes accompanied by at least one Hypomanic Episode." Bipolar II patients have very harsh depressions, and seem to enjoy their creative high moods. The highly productive person diagnosed with Bipolar II disorder usually has a genetic predisposition for this disorder (p. 359).

Cyclothymic Disorder: This is a milder form of bipolar illness characterized by chronic, unpredictable changes in mood for at least two years in adults and one year in children and adolescents. These numerous periods of hypomanic symptoms do not meet the criteria for a manic episode; and the depressive symptoms are not severe enough to meet the criteria for a major depressive episode. Symptom-free periods last no longer than two months in this period of time. During the initial two-year period in adults (one year in children and adolescents), no Manic Episode, Major Depressive Episode, or Mixed Episode have been present (p. 363).

54

Mood Episodes: Some of the common criteria for these four mood episodes (Manic, Major Depressive, Mixed, and Hypomanic) include:

(a) The symptoms manifested in each type of episode are severe enough to cause "marked impairment in occupational functioning or in usual social activities or relationships with others, or to necessitate hospitalization to prevent harm to self or others, or there are no psychotic symptoms".

(b) The symptoms exhibited in each type of episode "are not due to the direct physiological effects of a substance (e.g., a drug of abuse, a medication, or other treatment) or a general medical condition (e.g. hyperthyroidism)".

The DSM-IV criteria of these mood episodes occuring in Bipolar and Cyclothymic disorders are listed below.

Manic Episode: A "Manic Episode" is described as a clear cut period of "abnormally and persistently elevated, expansive, or irritable mood" for a period of a minimum of one week. Along with this "high" mood, at least 3 (or more) of the following symptoms must be present. Some of these may well be familiar to you (p. 332).

1. increased self-esteem (or grandiosity)
2. decreased need for sleep/full of energy
3. more talkative than usual; or with the need to talk in a pressing way flight of ideas, racing thoughts
4. easily distracted by unimportant or irrelevant external stimuli
5. increase in goal-directed activity (either socially, at work or school, or sexually) or psychomotor agitation
6. excessive involvement in pleasurable activities that have a high potential for painful consequences (e.g. foolish business ventures, sexual indiscretions, or unrestrained buying sprees)
7. These symptoms do not meet the criteria for a Mixed Episode

Hypomanic Episode: The Hypomanic Episode is a distinct period in which there is an abnormally and persistently elevated, expansive or irritable mood lasting at least for four days. This period of abnormal mood must be accompanied by at least three (or more) other manic symptoms listed above under Manic Episode.

A predictable indicator of the Hypomanic Episode is the decreased need for sleep (e.g. sleeping less than three hours per night). This episode is not severe enough to cause "marked impairment in social or occupational functioning (p. 338)."

Major Depressive Episode: The DSM-IV defines a "Major Depressive Episode" as characterized by a change from "normal" mood to a dysphoric mood and/or a loss of interest in usual activities. At least five of the following nine symptoms have been present *nearly every day* during the same two-week period. They represent a change from previous functioning; at least one of the symptoms is depressed mood or loss of interest or pleasure is necessary. Do you recognize any of them?

1. depressed mood most of the day (as indicated by subjective report or an observation made by others)

2. markedly diminished interest or pleasure in all, or almost all of the activities most of the day, or all day (as indicated by subjective report or an observation made by others)

3. significant weight gain or weight loss when not dieting (5% per month)/or change in appetite

4. sleep disturbances like insomnia or hypersomnia

5. slowing or agitation of mental and physical functioning as observed by others

6. chronic fatigue/decrease in energy

7. feelings of guilt, helplessness / hopelessness and worthlessness

8. indecisiveness, or decreased ability to concentrate (either by subjective account, or as observed by others)

9. frequent thoughts of death or suicide, or a suicide attempt

These symptoms do not meet the criteria for a Mixed Episode. Symptoms during a bereavement period are not diagnosed as a Major Depressive Episode unless the symptoms last longer than 2 months after a loss of a loved one (p. 327).

Mixed Episode: "The Mixed Episode" is characterized by a period of time (lasting at least one week) in which "the criteria are met both for a Manic Episode and for a Major Depressive Episode nearly every day during at least a 1-week period". Somatic antidepressant treatment (e.g. medication, electroconvulsive therapy, light therapy) clearly causing mixed-like episodes should not count toward a diagnosis of Bipolar I Disorder (p. 335).

Appendix II: The DSM-IV on Substance Dependence

The DSM-IV (p. 181) describes Substance Dependence as "a maladaptive pattern of substance use leading to clinically significant impairment or distress, as manifested by three (or more) of the following criteria occurring at any time in the same twelve month period:"

(1) Tolerance: Either a need for greater amounts of the substance to achieve the desired effects; or markedly decreased effect with continued use of the same amount of the substance. For example, when there has been cessation of alcohol in person dependent on alcohol, withdrawal symptoms can include increased hand tremor, sweating, insomnia, nausea and vomiting, hallucinations, anxiety, psychomotor agitation, or grand mal seizures.

(2) Withdrawal: When the substance use is stopped, a substance-specific syndrome develops; or the substance-specific syndrome can cause clinically significant distress or impairment in occupational or social areas of functioning not due to any other medical or mental disorder.

(3) The substance is taken over a longer period of time and in larger amounts than was originally intended.

(4) There is a continual desire or unsuccessful efforts made at cutting down or controlling the substance use.

(5) A great deal of time is spent in obtaining or using the substance or recovering from its effects.

(6) Social, recreational or occupational activities are given up or reduced because of substance use.

(7) Despite the knowledge that there is a recurrent physical or psychological problem caused by the substance, the use is continued.

Appendix III: Mood Stabilizers Used in the Co-occuring Disorders of Bipolar Disorder and Substance Dependence

Mood stabilizers:
Lithium

Tricyclic antidepressants (SSRI's):
Fluoxetine (Prozac)
Paroextine (Paxil)
Sertraline (Zoloft)

Newer anti-psychotic medications:
Olanzapine (Zyprexa)
Respiridone (Risperdal)
Quetiapine (Seroquel
Clozapine (Clozaril)
Bupropion (Wellbutrin)

Anticonvulsants:
The following anticonvulsant drugs have been shown to be effective in the treatment of the alcoholic patient having bipolar symptoms and in bipolar patients:
Divalproex (Depakote)
Tegretol (Carbamazepine)
Gabapentin (Neurontin)
Lamotrigine (Lamictal)
Valproic acid

Appendix IV: The Twelve Steps of
Alcoholics Anonymous (AA) in Relation to Adlerian Theory

These same "Twelve Steps" apply in principle to many self-help groups such as *Al-Anon; Alateen, Adult Children of Alcoholics, Cocaine Anonymous, Co-Anon, Nar-Anon, Narcotics Anonymous, Dual Recovery Anonymous, Gamblers Anonymous, Overeaters Anonymous*, to name a few. A fuller list, meeting schedules and directions to meetings can be found on the World Wide Web. Phone numbers can be obtained in the Yellow Pages of your phone book.

Ample evidence points to the effectiveness of these self-help programs, which are modeled on the pioneering work of Alcoholics Anonymous, and they have much in common with Adlerian principles. Like Adlerian psychology, Alcoholics Anonymous is a good example of social involvement that allows individuals to see themselves within a larger community. The 12-step programs can be wonderful precursors to the one-on-one experience that an Adlerian can later provide.

Step1: "We admitted we were powerless over alcohol — that our lives had become unmanageable."

In Step One of the 12-step program, the alcoholic/addict learns to admit how little control they have over their mood swings and drugs. They must break through the denial and begin to see that their lives have become a mess. Powerlessness is not in the Adlerian therapy vocabulary. However, Adlerians do use a paradoxical technique that allows the sufferer to admit he or she has a problem and now wants to do something about it. It is a indirect way of empowering the individual to trigger the start of the process of change.

Step 2: "We came to believe that a power greater than ourselves could restore us to sanity."

Step 3: "We made a decision to turn our will and lives over to the care of God as we understood him."

Most recovering patients have difficulty in the concepts of a Higher Power and spirituality presented in Steps Two and Three. The fifth life task in Adlerian psychology parallels the 12-step program in recognizing that recovering individuals need to recognize that they are not the center of the universe, but part of a larger whole. They can do this by identifying with a Higher Power and responding to their own spiritual needs. As this is a tall order during the early stages of recovery, some patients prefer to choose the power of the group, or the collective conscious of the group as the "Higher Power." In time, with more sobriety and lifestyle changes, recovering patients can become more aware of spiritual issues.

Step 4: *"We made a searching and fearless moral inventory of ourselves."*

Step 5: *"We admitted to God, to ourselves, and to another human being the exact nature of our wrongs."*

The fourth and fifth step of the 12-step program asks for a moral inventory to be drawn up and then admitted to openly. Acting on these steps can precipitate negative feelings and memories and is a painful stage for most. It can be a trigger for relapse, so most recovering people need a lot of outside support at this time. Many therapists suggest that those in recovery wait until they have a solid foundation and support system in place, probably after six months in the program, before attempting this.

As in Adlerian psychology, the recovering person is encouraged to become aware of all the trouble he or she has caused to self and those closest to him or her so that the old destructive faulty convictions and behaviors can be brought out in the open. These are preliminary steps towards reshaping his or her life.

Step 6: *"We were entirely ready to have remove these defects of character."*

Step 7: *"We humbly asked him to remove our shortcomings."*

Step 8: *"We made a list of all persons we had harmed, and became willing to make amends to them all."*

Step 9: *"We made direct amends to such people wherever possible, except when to do so would injure them or others."*

Steps 6 to 9 closely parallel the process of Adlerian therapy. Patients become aware of the mistakes they have made, take responsibility for past wrongdoings, understand how they made the mistakes, and look for ways to rectify the damage caused to others. Adlerians encourage their clients to reintegrate with the people closest to them by communicating, and making commitments to themselves and others around them. This helps them change defects in their personalities and they become less likely to make the same mistakes in the future. Turning to a Higher Power (even if is the higher power of the group at first) gives strength and encouragement to the recovering person. Adlerians believe that we are not alone in the grand scheme of life in this universe. We extend out from ourselves to our parents and relatives and friends and colleagues to the outside world and to the cosmos. In AA, people learn to extend out of themselves by interacting in their spiritual world of the AA group first, and then they can slowly reach out to the rest of the world and the cosmos.

Step 10: *"We continued to take a personal inventory and when we were wrong promptly admitted it."*

Step 11: *"We sought through prayer and meditation to improve our conscious contact with God as we understood him, praying only for knowledge of His will for us and the power to carry that out."*

Step 12: *"Having had a spiritual awakening as a result of these steps, we tried to carry this message to alcoholics, and to practice these principles in all our affairs."*

Steps 10 through 12 are about maintaining a changed lifestyle. These are highly Adlerian in nature. By focusing on his or her assets, the patient converts the pains of failure into optimistic cooperation with others. In our patient's life, the voice of the community has been silenced as he or she has spent more time with other alcoholics or addicts and avoided non-using family and friends. The 12-step programs help rebuild that lost sense of community and spirit, often among others also in recovery. Their recovery is fortified by helping newcomers take root in the program. At about this time, as the patient learns about their personal negative feelings and triggers, they know that there is a new community structure in place that can provide support and encouragement. Now the lifestyle work can proceed.

Appendix V: The Short-term and Long-term Side Effects of Mood-altering Chemicals

The short-term and long-term side effects of mood-altering drugs are classified here according to their central nervous system (CNS) depressant, stimulant or hallucinogenic properties. The CNS stimulant drugs include cocaine and the amphetamines. The CNS depressant-type drugs include alcohol, sedative-hypnotics, opiod analgesics, tranquilizers, inhalants and solvents. The hallucinogens are also referred to as psychedelic or mind-expanding drugs. We assign cannabis drugs a special category on their own (Section IV. Cannabinoids).

I.
CNS Depressants
Alcohol
Please refer to Chapter 7, p. 43 for a detailed description of the short-term and long-term effects of this "invisible" drug.

Opiod analgesics.
 These drugs are used medically for their pain-relief and cough-suppressant properties. They are classified as narcotics and include Opium, Morphine, Heroin, Codeine, Methadone, Demerol, Dilaudid, cough syrups (containing Codeine), Percodan, Darvon, Talwin, Lomotil, Butalbitol (containing codeine), Fiorinol-C. The opium-derived drugs are similar to the naturally occurring anti-pain pleasure compounds, endorphins, that act on the brain's opiate receptors. The short-term effects of the more common injectable forms of opiods include: a surge of pleasure (euphoria), a strong sense of well-being, and greatly diminished feelings of anxiety, hunger, sexual desire, depression and pain. The body feels warm and heavy, the mouth feels dry, the pupils of the eyes constrict to pinpoint. There is a tendency to nod while awake, with a daydreaming or glazed look on the face.

Other physical effects include: nausea, vomiting, increased urination, constipation, itchy skin, slowed breathing. In overdose, the skin becomes cold, moist, and bluish; breathing can come to a complete stop, resulting in death. As with injectable cocaine, the use of injected opiods can lead to the many complications listed above, including bruising, abscesses, brain damage and tetanus. Taken orally, the effects are more gradual. Opiods are extremely dangerous when used in combination with alcohol.

Long-term effects include severe constipation, moodiness and menstrual irregularities, lung problems, complications during pregnancy and birth. Narcotic drugs produce an intense physical dependence and it is extremely difficult to detoxify. Most addicts have to engage in some sort of criminal activity to afford their "fix". Tolerance develops rapidly, making higher doses necessary to achieve the desired effect. Withdrawal symptoms include: severe anxiety, insomnia, profuse sweating, shivering and chills, muscle spasms, tremors occurring 4 to 5 hours after last dose.

Sedative-Hypnotics

Sedative-hypnotics including Seconal, Nembuatl, Amytal, Tuinal, Mandrax (Quaaludes), Dalmane, Restoril, Rohypnol ("rodies" or "the forget pill") and Halcion. Their short term effects are in some ways similar to alcohol; that is, they slow down the central nervous system. Small doses relieve tension. Larger doses produce sleepiness, inattentiveness, slowed reflexes, blurred vision, staggering, impaired thinking, and reduced sensitivity to pain. Overdoses can cause a loss of consciousness, coma and death.

Long-term effects are: depression, impaired liver, headache, slurred speech and impaired vision. Tolerance and psychological dependence develops. Withdrawal symptoms are similar to those listed for alcohol. Taken together with alcohol, these drugs are dangerous and even fatal. Barbituate withdrawal is extremely dangerous with a high risk of fatal convulsions.

Other depressant psychotropic drugs:

GHB (gamma hydroxtbutyrate) (liquid Ecstasy) is popular at raves. It lowers inhibitions, causes euphoria, calmness leading to drowsiness, dizziness and amnesia. It has been used in sexual assaults and can easily be mistaken for water. GHB is similar to yet another brain chemical, GABA, gamma hydroxybutyric acid that acts on brain receptors and can cause hallucinations, tremors and seizures, nausea, vomiting, shortness of breath, loss of consciousness and coma in higher doses. Chronic use of GHB can lead to withdrawal symptoms.

Inhalants and Volatile Solvents

Some users resort to sniffing volatile hydrocarbons readily available in the open marketplace and sold as aerosols, paint thinners and removers, glue, plastic cement, nail polish removers, lighter fluid, cleaning fluids, and gasoline products. Inhaled vapors from solvents enter the bloodstream rapidly through the lungs and cause depression of the CNS. Short-term psychoactive effects include euphoria, lightheadedness, fantasizing and feelings of recklessness and bizarre behavior. Other physical effects are: slower heart rate and breathing, odor of the solvent on the breath, nausea, hallucinations, sneezing and coughing, increased salivation.

Larger doses may produce disorientation and unconsciousness, nosebleeds, red eyes, sores on the nose and mouth. Sniffing solvents can produce headaches and a hangover lasting several days. "Sudden sniffing death" can occur due to abnormalities caused to the heart during exercise or in a stressful situation. Situational hazards can cause burns, injury or death from fire or explosions. Suffocation can occur, especially if the user employs a plastic bag over the head to intensify the concentration of solvent sniffed.

Long-term effects of inhalant use include: forgetfulness, fatigue, weight loss, pallor, depression, tremors, irritability and an inability to think logically, and brain, liver and kidney impairment. Simultaneous alcohol ingestion can cause further damage to these organs. Tolerance, psychological and physical dependence develops with regular use. Withdrawal symptoms are similar to those listed for alcohol and other CNS depressants.

Tranquilizers

Tranquilizers are CNS depressants that produce calm without causing actual sleep. They are used to counteract anxiety and nervousness. They include the benzodiazepines: Valium, Serax, Ativan, and Xanax. Relaxed muscle tension, loss of inhibition, reduced mental alertness, feelings of well-being, mild impairment of balance, nausea, rash, and dizziness are some of the short-term effects.

These drugs become hazardous when taken with alcohol, other sedatives or cold, cough or allergy remedies. The long-term effects of tranquilizers include: disorientation, impairment of logical thoughts, memory and judgment. There are further hazards to pregnant women and the fetus. As with the other CNS depressants, tolerance, psychological and physical dependence, and withdrawal symptoms can develop.

II.
Stimulants

Central nervous system stimulants cause the release of noradrenaline and other chemical messengers like dopamine and serotonin (neurotransmitters) that stimulate the sympathetic nervous system. The stimulation felt after ingesting one of these chemicals is the result of increased release of these neurotransmitters working on the nervous system. The effect is a temporary feeling of wakefulness and happiness. The noradrenaline release is very similar to the excitation of being in an emergency in a "fight or flight" situation. Because stimulants provide a sense of increased physical and mental energy, the rush of excitement they produce is very tempting to some individuals.

Other physical effects are an increase in heart rate and blood pressure. Fingertips can become cold due to the changes in blood circulation. These drugs can also cause nervousness, an increase in the rate of breathing, stomach irritation in the form of indigestion, increased urine production and a laxative effect. Dependence can develop if the person develops a bad relationship with any of these substances. Withdrawal symptoms may include headaches, fatigue, and depression.

Caffeine
Please refer to Chapter 7, p. 41 for a description of the short-term and long-term effects of this "invisible" drug.

Nicotine
See Chapter 7, p. 42 for a complete list of the short-term and long-term effects of this "invisible" drug.

Cocaine.
Coca leaves chewed by many in South America contains 14 ingredients, the most important one is cocaine. Extracted from coca leaves, pure cocaine is mixed with a white powder like cornstarch or sugar (anywhere from 5% to 80% cocaine), and inhaled ("snorted") to produce an intense if short-lived effect on the brain. Refined cocaine is more potent in smaller quantities, and more toxic, than leaves.

Like all stimulant-type drugs, cocaine also acts on the pleasure pathway in the brain at the ends of the nerve cells (synapses) that release messenger molecules called dopamine. The released dopamine stimulates an electrical signal on the receiver neuron. Normally the dopamine, once released, finds its way back to the original transmitting nerve cell to be recycled. However, cocaine blocks this recycling route, so the resulting effect is an accumulation of dopamine at the receiver neuron, causing an over-stimulation of the receiver nerve cell and the "rush" or "high" in the cocaine user. The intense feeling of euphoria so produced is of shorter duration than the narcotic drugs.

Other short-term effects include: a feeling of enhanced physical strength and mental capacity with a sense of less fatigue, reduced need for food or sleep, restlessness, difficulties in concentration, sudden fatigue (in rebound as the nerve endings are depleted of the dopamine or neurotransmitter). Like caffeine and nicotine, its physical effects include: an increase in the heart rate and blood pressure; faster breathing, sweating, a rise in body temperature, dilatation of the pupils, pallor. Large doses of cocaine lead to erratic or violent behavior, blurred vision, and convulsions. "Crack" is the smokable, so-called freebase form of cocaine. It can reach the brain in 8 seconds. Injectable cocaine reaches the brain in 15 seconds.

Cocaine not only affects the brain cells, but many other systems in the body. Some long-term effects are: insomnia, chronic running nose, inability to smell, angina, irregular heart beat, heart attacks, and sometimes death in persons vulnerable to cardiovascular abnormalities, arterial constriction or aneurysm leading to stroke, tremors, grand mal seizures (that in themselves can lead to death), psychoses, accumulation of fluid in the lungs, damage to the lining in the nasal septum due to snorting, impotence, constipation. Other organ damage from chronic use includes irritation of the respiratory tract leading to infections such as bronchitis and allergic reactions to the street preparations.

The chronic cocaine user can develop paranoid psychosis, which can lead to extreme antisocial behavior. Its use can lead to weight loss, and deterioration of the nervous system. There are many fetal risks in the pregnant mother, including miscarriage, premature birth and stillbirth. Also, the pregnant cocaine user bears a baby with possible retarded growth, stiff limbs, hyper-irritability, increased chance of crib death, strokes and seizures. The injectable cocaine has many of its own long-term side effects related to syringe and needle use. These include: pulmonary embolism (a blood clot in the pulmonary artery); bacterial endocarditis (infected heart valves); hepatitis and AIDS; meningitis (fatal brain infection); phlebitis (blood clot in the leg).

Cocaine is psychologically habit forming. Withdrawal symptoms include restlessness, paranoia and depression.

Amphetamines

Amphetamines (Benzedrine, Dexedrine (dexies), and Methedrine (speed), are synthetic CNS stimulant drugs (i.e. manufactured through chemical means), derived from chemicals related to the hormone adrenaline. They are usually taken orally as pills and improve physical and mental performance. In the early 1960's, doctors did not hesitate to prescribe amphetamines to make people productive and happy.

Many of the short-term and long-term effects of amphetamines are similar to that of cocaine. They raise the blood pressure, increase heart rate, heighten mental alertness, and reduce hunger. With prolonged use, amphetamine abuse can lead to extreme irritability, paranoia, violence, kidney damage, lung problems, stroke, malnutrition, and amphetamine psychosis.

Others in the stimulant category include Ritalin—(methylphenidate), diethylpropion (Tenuate), and Phentermine.

III.
Hallucinogens

LSD
Lysergic acid diethylamide is the most potent of the semi-synthetic hallucinogens. It acts on the brain to cause sensory distortions to sight, sound, touch, smell and taste. It has a chemical structure is very similar to the brain neurotransmitter, serotonin. LSD stimulates the serotonin receptors of the brain neurons, causing vivid visual and even auditory hallucinations. Individual responses to LSD can vary greatly. Short-term effects include extreme mood swings and users sometimes experience several different emotions at the same time. Effects can include aggression, terror, impairment in concentration and loss of short-term memory. Users may lose their sense of identity through LSD use. Feelings of unreality, depression, anxiety and even panic can occur. These are typical of the "bad trip".

Other physical effects of LSD include: muscle weakness, trembling, increased blood pressure, rapid breathing, nausea, and chills. Long-term effects include: decreased motivation, flashbacks long after the drug is taken, prolonged   depression, anxiety and other psychotic reactions like acute schizophrenia, brain damage, increased risk of spontaneous abortion and other fetal damage in pregnant mothers on hallucinogens.

Other hallucinogens acting in much the same manner as LSD include: PCP (angel dust), a dangerous potent hallucinogen almost guaranteed to cause a bad trip; MDA; MDMA (Ecstasy); mescaline or peyote; psilocybin (magic mushrooms); morning glory seeds, STP or DOM; PMA; DMT; and 2-CB (also known as 2C-B). These hallucinogens produce tolerance that may cross over from one hallucinogen to another. They also cause psychological dependence, but not physical dependence.

The most popular hallucinogen used at the all-night raves is the stimulant MDMA, better known as Ecstasy. It can also be widely misrepresented and impure, coming in many different types of packaging (M&M's, Skittles, multi-colored tablets possibly containing a whole mix of stimulants like MDA, PMA, and caffeine. Ecstasy, also called the "love drug", produces an increase in body temperature (hyperthermia) and heart rate, teeth grinding, anxiety, memory impairment, nausea, heart attacks, liver and kidney damage, strokes, seizures, a long hangover consisting of muscle aches, irritability, insomnia, confusion, paranoia, memory impairment and depression lasting for days or weeks. Ecstasy-related dehydration can lead to kidney or heart failure and even death. Like other stimulants, dangers increase if a person has depression or psychoses, diabetes, asthma, epilepsy or an impaired heart.

IV.
Cannabinoids

Cannabis preparations include marijuana, hashish, hash oil, and THC (tetrahydrocannibinol). In all, THC is the main psychoactive ingredient. Cannabinoids, an unusual class of drugs, are not labeled in the stimulant or depressant categories of psychoactive drugs. Depending on drug experience of the user, on the mind set, and on the setting in which the user smokes marijuana, this drug has mixed stimulant, depressant, hallucinogenic and psychedelic properties. Cannabis users who want to relax, and place themselves in a peaceful environment, may well relax. On the other hand, for party-goers, marijuana can act as a stimulant. Besides relaxation, other short-term effects of marijuana are: increased appetite and feelings of euphoria.

Marijuana is a product of the hemp plant and has been used since prehistoric times. Its effects are: lightheadedness, a sense of well being, heightened attention to one's perception of things and an increased awareness to inner mental events. Sharpened sensations and other mild internal cognitive events are also present. At larger doses, perceptions of time, sound, color and shape may be distorted. These milder effects often give way to perceptual alterations of things that often develop into vivid imagery. Finally, that imagery can blossom into a hallucination. Emotions are intensified through the use of marijuana and those emotions can include a sense of mild euphoria or apathy, serenity, or anxiety.

Apathy, impaired coordination and balance, reduction in logical thinking and impaired motor skills can result from smoking. This is especially true when marijuana is combined with other depressant-type drugs such as alcohol, barbiturates (sleeping pills) and tranquilizers. There are cases of bad reactions in larger doses producing anxiety, panic, or even psychotic episodes, due to resulting confusion, excitement and hallucinations. Some other short-term physical effects include: red eyes, dry mouth and throat.

Cannabis long-term effects include short-term memory and motivational loss. Four to ten times more tar is produced from burning cannabis when compared to tobacco. Chronic bronchitis and a higher risk of lung cancer are major long-term consequences from marijuana smoking. The normal development of the fetus may be negatively affected if a pregnant mother smokes. There can be a reduction in male testosterone levels, chromosomal damage, and reduced immunity to infections. Psychological dependence develops in regular users. Withdrawal symptoms include loss of appetite, nervousness, anxiety, sweating, and sleep disturbances. With long-term use of cannabis, tolerance develops.

Bibliography and Resources

Theory

Addiction Research Foundation of Ontario. (1981). *Facts about drugs.* Toronto: Author.

Adler, A. (1935). What is neurosis? *International Journal of Individual Psychology*, 1, 9-17.

Altus, W. (1972). Birth order and its sequelae. In U. Bronfenbrenner (Ed.), *Influences on human development* (pp. 600-611). Hinsdale, IL: The Dryden Press Inc.

American Psychiatric Association. (1994). *Diagnostic and statistical manual of mental disorders* (4th ed.). Washington, D.C: Author.

Andreasen, N. & Glick, I. (1988). Bipolar affective disorder and creativity: Implications and clinical management. *Comprehensive Psychiatry*, 29, 207-217.

Angier, N. (1993, October 12). Old idea about creativity and madness wins new scientific support. *The New York Times.*

Ansbacher, H. & Ansbacher, R. (Eds.) (1956). *The Individual Psychology of Alfred Adler: A systematic presentation in selections from his writings.* New York: Basic Books.

Ansbacher, H. & Ansbacher, R. (Eds.) (1964). *Superiority and social interest: A collection of later writings.* New York: W.W. Norton and Company.

Ansbacher, H. (1974). Goal-oriented Individual Psychology: Alfred Adler's theory. In A. Burton (Ed.), *Operational theories of personality.* New York: Brunner/Mazel Publishers.

Ansbacher, H. (1991). The concept of social interest. *Individual Psychology*, 47, 28- 46.

Corsini, R. (Ed.) (1984). *Current psychotherapies.* Itsaca: F.E. Peacock Publishers.

DeAngelis, T. (1989). Mania, depression and genius. *The A.P.A Monitor*, 20, 1-24.

Dreikurs, R. & Soltz, V. (1964). *Children: The Challenge*. New York: Hawthorn.

Duffy, W. (1975). *Sugar blues*. New York: Warner Books Inc.

Hirschfeld, R., Calabrese, J., Weissman, M., Reed, M., Davies, M., Frye, M., Keck, P., Lewis, L., McElroy, S., McNulty, J., & Wagner, K. (2003). Screening for bipolar disorder in the community. *J. Clin. Psychiatry*, 64(1), 53-59

Holden, C. (1987, April). Creativity and the troubled mind. *Psychology Today*, p.9.

Jamison, K. (1993). *Touched with fire: Manic-depressive illness and the artistic temperament*. New York: Free Press Paperbacks.

Ludwig, A. (1994). Mental illness and creative activity in female writers. *Amer. J. of Psychiatry*, 151, 1650-1656.

Mosak, H. (1977). *On purpose: Collected papers*. Chicago: Alfred Adler Institute.

Mozdzierz, G. (1996). Adler's "What is neurosis?": Clinical and predictive revelations from the past. *Individual Psychology*, 52 (4), 342-350.

Nystul, M.S. (1993). The Nystul turning point survey: An assessment instrument to analyze Adlerian tasks of life. *Individual Psychology*, 49, 185-198.

Post, F. (1994). Creativity and psychopathology: A study of 291 world-famous men. *Br. J. of Psychiatry*, 165, 22-34.

Schildkraut, J., Hirshfield, A. & Murphy, J. (1994). Mind and mood in modern art: Depressive disorders, spirituality, and early deaths in the abstract expressionist artist of the New York school. *Am. J. of Psychiatry*, 151, 482-488.

Shulman, B. & Mosak, H. (1988). *Manual for life style assessment.* Muncie: Accelerated Development Inc.

Stein, H. (1997, June 20). *Classical Adlerian Psychotherapy.* Retrieved February 1, 2002, from http://www.behavior.net

Weil, A. & Rosen, W. (1983). *Chocolate to Morphine: Understanding mind-active drugs.* Boston: Houghton Mifflin Publishers.

Treatment

Al-Anon Family Group Headquarters, Inc. (1991). *Al-Anon Family Groups: Formerly, Living with an alcoholic.* New York: Author.

Alcoholics Anonymous World Services, Inc. (1976). *Alcoholics Anonymous - The Big Book: The story of how many thousands of men and women have recovered from alcoholism* (3rd ed.). New York: Author.

Center for Addiction and Mental Health. (2000). *Bipolar Disorder: An information guide.* Toronto: Author.

Dreikurs, R. (1997). Holistic Medicine. *Individual Psychology,* 53, 128-205.

Fieve, R. (1997). *Moodswing* (2nd ed.). New York: Bantam Books.

Ginther, C. (1999). Schuckit addresses state-of-the-art addiction treatments. *Psychiatric Times,*16(4). Retrieved August 20, 2003, from http://www.psychiatrictimes.com/p990457.html

Hazelden Publications (1993). *The dual diagnosis recovery book: A twelve step program for those of us with addiction and an emotional or psychiatric illness.* Center City: Author.

Hobson, J. & Leonard, J. (2001). *Out of its mind: Psychiatry in crisis: A call for reform.* Cambridge, Mass: Perseus Publishing.

Howard, K., Lueger, R., Mailing, M. & Martinovitch, Z. (1993). A phase model of psychotherapy outcome: Causal mediation of change. *Journal of Consulting and Clinical Psychology,* 61, 678-685.

Korenberg, M. & Tafler, D. (1978). *Trapped: The fraud of mental illness* (2nd ed.). Montreal: Kay-Rakier Incorporated.

Lewis, J. & Carlson, J. (1996). Substance abuse treatment and Individual Psychology. In L. Sperry & J.Carlson (Eds.), *From DSM- IV Diagnosis to treatment* (2nd ed., pp. 353-369). Washington, D.C: Accelerated Development Inc.

Longo, L. & Bohn, M. (2001). Alcoholism pharmacotherapy: New approaches to an old disease. *Hospital Physician*, June 2001, 33-43.

Mozdzierz, G. & Greenblatt, R. (1994). Technique in psychotherapy: Cautions and concerns. *Individual Psychology*, 50, 232-249.

Pancner, R. (1996). Depressive disorders. In L. Sperry & J. Carlson (Eds.), *From DSM- IV Diagnosis to treatment* (2nd ed., pp.115-157). Washington, D.C: Accelerated Development Inc.

Pevin, D. (1996). Individual psychology and bipolar mood disorder. In L. Sperry & J. Carlson (Eds.), *From DSM- IV diagnosis to treat ment* (2nd ed., pp.77-114). Washington, D.C: Accelerated Development Inc.

Pevin, D. & Shulman, B. (1983). The psychodynamics of bipolar affective disorder: Some empirical findings and their implications for cognitive therapy. *Individual Psychology*, 39, 2-16.

Prinz, J. (1993). Alcoholics and their treatment: Current Adlerian thinking. *Individual Psychology*, 49, 94-105

Seligman, M. (1991). *Learned optimism*. New York: Alfred A. Knopf.

Seligman, M. (1995). The effectiveness of psychotherapy: The consumer reports study. *American Psychologist*, 50, 965-974.

Sperry, L. & Carlson, J. (Eds.) (1996). *Psychopathology and psychotherapy: From DSM- IV diagnosis to treatment* (2nd ed.). Washington, D.C: Accelerated Development Inc.

Weiss, R. (1999, April 28). Mood disorders and substance abuse: Highlights of a MDDA-Boston lecture. Retrieved May 21, 2003, from http://www.mmdaboston.org/Lect042899.html.

Westermeyer, J., Ziedonis, D. & Weiss, R. (Eds.) (2003). *Integrated treatment of mood and substance use disorders.* Baltimore: John's Hopkins University Press.

Family Literature

Al-Anon Family Group Headquarters, Inc. (1991). *Al-Anon Family Groups: Formerly, "Living with an alcoholic".* New York, N.Y: Author

Al-Anon Family Group Headquarters, Inc. (1977). *What's "Drunk," Mama?* New York, N.Y: Author.

Beattie, M. (2000). *Codependent No More* (15th ed.). Center City: Hazelden Publications.

Typpo, M. (1984). *An elephant in the living room: The children's book.* Center City: Hazelden Publications.

Woititz, J. (1983). *Adult children of alcoholics.* Pompano Beach: Health Communications, Inc.

Helplines and Websites for people in treatment along with their families

Co-Anon Family Groups (2003). Retrieved on September 8, 2003, from www.co-anon.org

Cocaine Anonymous World Services (2001). Retrieved on September 8, 2003, from www.ca.org

Drug, Alcohol and Mental Health Information Line: 1-800-463-6273.

Health Canada, Minister of Public Works and Government Services (2000). *Straight Facts about Drugs and Drug Abuse* [Electronic version]. Retrieved July 22, 2003, from http://www.hc-sc.gc.ca/hecs-sesc/cds/pdf/straight_facts.pdf

Health Canada (2003). *Canadian Health Network: Information You Can Trust.* Retrieved December 28, 2003 from http://www.canadian-health-network.ca

Hope and help for families and friends of alcoholics (2003). Retrieved July 22, 2003, from Al-Anon Family Group Headquarters web site: http:// www.al-anon.org/hope.html

International Substance Abuse Resources: 1-800-662-HELP (4357).

Narcotics Anonymous World Services, Inc. (1999). Retrieved July 22, 2003, from http://www.na.org

National Alliance for the Mentally Ill about Substance Abuse and Mood Disorders (2003). Retrieved on July 22, 2003, from http://www.psycom.net/depression.central.substance.html

National Cocaine Hotline: 1-800-COCAINE.

Raves: Exploring today's counter culture (2003). Retrieved August 20, 2003, from Cincinnati Children's Hospital Medical Center web site: http://www.cincinnatichildren's.org/cgi-bin

Recovery Resources Online. Retrieved December 28th, 2003, from http://www.soberrecovery.com/links/resources.html

The Twelve Traditions of Dual Recovery Anonymous (2003). Retrieved August 20, 2003, from Dual Recovery Anonymous website: http://www.draonline.org/dra_trads.html

Welcome to Alcoholics Anonymous Alcoholics (2003). Retrieved on July 22, 2003, from Alcoholics Anonymous World Services website: http://www.alcoholics-anonymous.org

Biographical and other Research Material

Hoffman, E. (1994). *The drive for self: Alfred Adler and the founding of Individual Psychology.* Reading: Addison-Wesley Publishing Company.

Stotland, M. (1990). *The life style analysis of John Lennon.* Unpublished M.A. Counseling Psychology thesis, Alfred Adler Institute of Chicago, Chicago, IL.

About the Authors

Dr. Marlene Stotland Cohen has followed two careers, as a pharmacologist (McGill University), and as a psychotherapist (Alfred Adler Institute of Chicago). Her area of specialization is in helping people with substance abuse issues, which draws upon both fields of her expertise. She worked for 10 years at a treatment center for alcoholism and drug addiction where she headed the group therapy and family counseling aspect of the program. She discovered that recovering patients had the greatest success in their treatment when they started to understand the cognitive processes that undermine them. Many in this client group also had some form of mood disorder. There was a higher success rate with those that tackled family alienation brought about by their substance dependence. Dr. Stotland Cohen is in private practice in Montreal.

Over the past 40 years, *Dr. Gerald J. Mozdzierz* has dedicated himself to helping others afflicted with mental as well as physical illness. He is a Professor of Psychiatry and Behavioral Neuroscience at Loyola University Stritch School of Medicine, a Fellow of the American Academy of Clinical Psychology, and a Diplomate of the American Board of Professional Psychology. He has published countless papers in professional journals of psychology, medicine and ethics, presented papers at national and international meetings and served as editor to the Journal of Individual Psychology. He has also given innumerable workshops and courses in psychology across North America and Europe.